BEYOND REASONABLE DOUBT

An investigation of Spiritual Truths and Myths

by

Trevor Davey

With acknowledgments to all those who have provided information and guidance over the years. To my Spirit Mentors, for providing information and inspiration. Also, to my wife Lucy for giving me ideas and suggestions together with proof reading the text.

CON-PSY PUBLICATIONS

First Edition

Published by
CON-PSY PUBLICATIONS

P.O. BOX 14,
GREENFORD,
MIDDLESEX, UB6 0UF.

ISBN 978 1 898680 59 8

CONTENTS

Introduction to a way of thinking

The objective of this book is to make suggestions as to how Spirit Energies communicate with those in the Physical Realms. Clearly there are no definitive formulae for spirit communication and there are numerous examples of the way Spirit Energies, of those who reside in the Spiritual Realms, help and guide us mere mortals. Very few people profess to have a total understanding of the ability of Spirit Mentors to guide, support and influence our physical existence. Many will, of course, vehemently argue that there is no life after life, let alone Spirit Mentors to help us as and when needed. There are also many who, especially in the arts, accept that they receive inspiration in some form without realising that this may be influence generated by Spirit Energies.

Those who are fortunate enough to have an understanding of the eternal progress of every human soul are truly blessed and knowing that Spirit Energy is an intrinsic part of the human body, they accept that our spirit friends progress and willingly offer their help. Throughout the philosophy and theology understandings of the human race there is an acceptance of eternal life in all religions. Spiritualism, in all its various doctrines, aims to understand fully the activities of the Spiritual Realms. Although there is a common theme of eternal progress, there are many variations on the understanding portrayed.

So, how did my journey of understanding and development of mediumship progress over nearly 70 years of life in this Physical Existence happen? Firstly, I was born into a family of Spiritualists, whether by choice or design remains a mystery at this time. My maternal grandfather was a Minister, speaker and demonstrator as well as a trance and transfiguration medium. My father was also a platform medium and a Minister. My mother was more interested in philosophy and speaking and writing on spiritual understanding and the work of the Spiritualist Lyceum Union. She was also ordained as a Minister of the Spiritualist National Union. I suppose you could say it was in my DNA to work for Spirit in my own way.

As a child I remember seeing Spirit and, I am told, conversing and playing with a young female spirit child. However, this early ability to communicate was lost for nearly 50 years. My late first wife, Eileen, was brought up in a Spiritualist family and we both attended the Spiritualist Lyceum and Church in Hounslow, West London. When our daughter Judith came along, the involvement with Spiritualism and spiritual development took second place to bringing her up, as well as career development. In the 1980s we were invited to join a development group to train as Spiritual Healers. This group, apart from development of healing, was also a Physical Circle with all sorts of physical activity happening in the séance environment. This included footsteps, bells ringing, sand writing, automatic writing, movement of objects and actual physical manifestations where the spirit energy became noticeable - the energy being felt by the sitters as solid bodies. We were also given trance teachings from various Spirit Energies for our further understanding. During this time Eileen became aware of her hands and arms being moved when she was in meditation in the circle and we were aware that this could be the first stages of trance communication.

Away from the circle environment, in our own home, under controlled conditions, the development of trance communication quickly began. At first, it was just a few words and then it became a torrent of information. Much of this communication was published in various spiritual journals and later in three books: 'Words of Wisdom' (1998), 'Go Forward to a New Millennium' (1999) and 'Further Words of Wisdom' (2001). Apart from Home Circles, public demonstrations became possible at many venues in this country and abroad, coupled with a workshop on spiritual matters. Sometime before there was any indication that Eileen was to develop a serious terminal illness, whilst in trance, her main guide Mafra (a Portuguese wine grower and merchant who lived in Porto) came through announcing that they were transferring the ability for channelling philosophy, under trance conditions, to myself. At this time I had some limited mental mediumship and worked as a Spiritual Healer - I always considered that my role was to present our workshops and ensure Eileen's safety whilst working in trance. After Eileen's passing to the Higher Realms, my abilities for trance and mental mediumship progressed, the latter flourishing only after I had sat under the guidance of my then Circle Leader, Brenda Harrison and her spirit helpers. Eventually I was to marry again, to Lucy, who is a Spiritual Healer, Reiki Master, Crystal Healer and has an extensive knowledge of spiritual understandings, as well as abilities to communicate with Spirit.

Since 2010, we have prepared articles published in the *Psychic World* newspaper, titled 'Joining in a Traditional Home Circle', recording the philosophy given and the questions asked of the Spirit Teachers and their answers. These are, as far as possible, verbatim, however, there is always a problem in converting the spoken words taking into account the intonation, speed of delivery and pauses for emphasis, to ensure that persons not in attendance at the circle can understand the words being given.

With this background, I trust that I can offer my readers some further understanding of spiritual matters and the communication of Spirit in its many forms. I do not aim to dictate what is absolute and total knowledge because this is, I believe, beyond the ability of our physical brain to comprehend. However, I do aim to bring food for thought and suggestions for everyone to take forward in their own path of understanding.

Why do we need Spiritualist Churches/Centres and Congregations?

Before the advent of formalised groups of like-minded people, spiritual communication took place in people's homes and as a sort of entertainment for the curious. It was, therefore, important for these groups who had a common interest to establish some form of organisation to set standards and to discover the most appropriate way of presenting spiritual phenomena and philosophy. The establishing of a formal organisation with a constitution is necessary for a business to function, manage its financial affairs and own property. In the UK, this also now includes registration with the Charity Commission for larger organisations. There are two distinct groups of Spiritualist organisations: One that accepts Jesus Christ as the Saviour of Mankind and the other group, who accept Jesus Christ as a wonderful medium and healer from whose philosophy much can be learnt.

Spiritualist services vary from organisation to organisation and normally follow a set pattern for Divine Services rather than Mediumistic Demonstration. The standard programme consists of prayers and the sending out of healing energies to those listed in the Healing Book. Then a philosophy, or spiritually based reading, followed by an address - possibly based on the reading, then a demonstration of spirit communication, all linked together with hymns or songs. In some services there may be a period of lead meditation, a soloist or choir singing, musical interlude, communion (in some Christian Spiritualist Churches) and spiritual hands-on healing incorporated into the service. In the early days of Spiritualism (from the late 1800s) the formal services were based around other religious organisations and their ways of doing things, with a probable major influence of the Wesleyan (later Methodist) service.

In the past, the congregation would be invited to ask the visiting speaker/medium questions on spiritual understanding matters towards the end of the service.

Today, there is a level of control on the way Spiritualism is portrayed, especially ensuring that spirit communication is primarily for 'proof of survival', encouragement and greetings from loved ones from the Higher Realms. The offering of predictions or 'fortune telling', as well as medical diagnosis and suggestions of medication, is not considered correct and is in certain circumstances illegal and places the medium in an unenviable position if things go wrong or complaints are made.

It is worth at this juncture considering what Spirit can predict. Spirit is aware of the circumstances around the person receiving a message from a medium, together with their medical condition. They are also aware of other conditions around that person and can, therefore, be aware of the bigger picture. One example is that Spirit will be aware that a lady is expecting a child before the woman herself knows. This is because they are aware of the spiritual energy, or soul, co-joining with the biological embryo to form the new physical life.

Some of the Historical Evidence

There is nothing new in the acceptance of a spiritual existence and the ability of humans to seek help from Spirit Energies, in whatever way they are understood in different cultures, creeds and religions. We know of stories handed down about ancient cultures seeking to contact their ancestors for help and guidance. They achieved this ability to communicate with Spirit by means of rituals, chanting and dances and possibly by the use of natural hallucinogenic herbs to put them into a form of trance. However, they could have just been natural mediums.

There is one school of thought supported by teachings from Spirit that all living creatures have a natural ability to communicate with Spirit Energies - you only have to study your pet cat or dog to realise that they have some form of knowing! An example of this is if a pet dog or cat is present when spiritual healing or mediumistic activities are taking place; the animal will react in a way that they would not in normal circumstances. This can indicate that they are aware of Spirit Energies being close. Of course, the ancient Egyptians were well aware of the psychic abilities of cats. It would seem that over the centuries of human evolvement the general ability to communicate at a higher level has been subdued and needs to be reawakened if the ability to communicate with Spirit is desired. We are told that spirit communication takes place in the third part of the brain at the rear of the scull - the cerebellum. It is interesting to note that the shape of the scull in ancient man was in a shape that could accommodate a larger cerebellum. Did this indicate a larger brain mass to convert spirit vibrations in an easier and natural way?

There are many examples of spirit communication in the Old and New Testaments of the Holy Bible, although we know that the providence of these reports relies on teachings being handed down the centuries by the storytellers, philosophers, thinkers, teachers and theologians before being transferred into written word, with some political interference, especially with the New Testament. The basic biblical reports are generally accepted as 'gospel' but unfortunately much of the detail is lost. Can you imagine how these events would have been recorded today with eye witness accounts, medical expert opinion on the miracles portrayed, together with detailed chapter and verse? The investigations held, rightly and properly by the Roman Catholic Church, into purported healing miracles at Lourdes (France) and Fatima (Portugal) come to mind in ensuring that there is no explanation other than the Will of God.

When we get to more recent times, the recording of spirit activity has a much better providence. The experiences of the following spirit communication are given as examples and are by no means complete:

Emmanuel Swedenborg – He was born in 1688 and his father was an army chaplain who was later to become chaplain to the Swedish Royal Family. Emmanuel had a very good education for those times in medicine, astronomy, mathematics, natural sciences, Latin and Greek. Later on, he was renowned for his mechanical inventions together with his theories about the working of the cerebral cortex and pituitary glands in the human body (which we now consider to have links with the ability for spirit communication). He also developed 'trance mediumship' and through this ability was given a great insight into the understanding of the Gospels and many other things long before they became the general understanding. As a prolific writer of many published works, he is still a source of knowledge and these works have been translated into many languages. The Swedenborg Society was established in 1810 and is still active at their premises in Bloomsbury, London. The providence for his links with Spirit are very well respected as the knowledge given was 'new knowledge'. His links with the Swedish Royal family and his personal standing were exceptional. There is an understanding that one of the spirit inspirers of Andrew Jackson Davis was Emmanuel Swedenborg.

Andrew Jackson Davis - (AJD) was born in 1826 in Blooming Grove (Orange County), N.Y. (USA) and had very little schooling. In 1843, his family moved to Poughkeepsie. In 1843, he attended a lecture on Mesmerism and a short time later he met William Livingstone who was experimenting with Mesmerism. AJD found that he was clairvoyant and could obtain knowledge from a higher plane of existence. He was able to read closed books and could diagnose illnesses and prescribe treatments that were generally effective. He claimed he was able to visit the Spiritual Realms in a trance state and he wrote extensively on his findings, including Divine Truths and the Laws of the Universe. He was able to comprehend how children, who have passed to the Spirit Realms at a young age, were taught. This became the basis of the formation of Lyceums, to teach children spiritual truths and good citizenship. The Lyceum movement in the UK and to a lesser extent in other parts of the world, still flourishes, although it now encompasses all ages seeking enlightenment, under the banner of The Spiritualist Lyceum Union.

His first book, 'Principles of Nature', about his communication with the Spiritual Realms, was published in 1847 and evidently up to this time he only had about five months formal schooling. He eventually wrote and published over 30 books in 45 editions. In 1844, AJD claimed to have been transported by what today we would term 'Astral Travel', to the Catskill Mountains where he met the Greek physician Galen and the Swedish seer Emanuel Swedenborg, both having passed many years previously. AJD also predicted the advent of what today we term 'Spiritualism'. It is thought that he had links with Abraham Lincoln, the United States of America President at the time of the American Civil War, who was involved with the abolition of slavery in parts of the American continent. Later in his life Andrew acquired a medical degree and opened a small shop, selling books and prescribing herbal remedies for his patients. He passed in 1910 and his burial stone can still be seen in a graveyard in Boston, Massachusetts (USA). He is often referred to as the "Poughkeepsie's Seer".

The Wesley Family – The parents of John Wesley (founder of the Methodist Church) lived in the Rectory at

Epworth in North Lincolnshire where his father Samuel Wesley was the rector. In December 1716, the family experienced the phenomena of spirit rappings, similar to those experienced by the Fox Sisters some years later. Footsteps were also heard, as well as bottles breaking and a bag of coins being emptied. These activities lasted for about two months and then occasionally over the years. The family called the energy causing these phenomena "Old Jeffrey", although there is no record of an intelligent interface being established. The providence for these happenings is based on a letter by Emily Wesley (one of John Wesley's sisters), dated 16 February 1750, containing the passage: "Another thing is that wonderful thing called by us Jeffrey. You won't laugh at me for being superstitious if I tell you how certainly that something calls on me against any extraordinary new affliction; but so little is known of the invisible world that I am at least not able to judge whether it be a friendly or an evil spirit". There are also the well-written notes by Mrs Wesley (The Rector's wife), recording the events. It is interesting to speculate that if the family had used the same techniques as the Fox Sisters to communicate with Old Jeffrey, modern Spiritualism may have started 121 years earlier.

The Fox Sisters - On the night of 31st March 1848, what is known as the 'Hydesville Rappings' began to happen in the Fox family's small country home, in the small town of Hydesville, New York State (USA) and witnessed by the Fox sisters. The two younger daughters managed to form a system of communication with the energy they coined as "Mr Splitfoot" by clapping their hands and asking Mr Splitfoot to make the same number of raps. Eventually they were able to have an intelligent communication which identified the spirit energy as a peddler who had died and was incarcerated within the walls of the house. Some years later the body of a man was found within the walls of the building. These events are considered to be the start of modern Spiritualism and at a later date Spiritualist meetings were started and became very popular. Gradually the faith of Spiritualism evolved with formal meeting places and churches. Abraham Lincoln met the Fox sisters and with the links with AJD became an ardent Spiritualist.

Alfred Russell Wallace (1823 -1913) - He was a British naturalist, explorer, geographer, anthropologist and biologist. He is best known for independently proposing a theory of evolution due to natural selection that prompted Charles Darwin to publish his own theory. As a scientist, he recorded his findings in a detailed manner, exploring all possible explanations in a logical fashion so that others could follow his ideas. In 1870, he became interested in the emerging activities of Spiritualists. He attended many séances with the well-known mediums of the time and witnessed many forms of communication, including materialisation, table movement, spirit photography (photographs that when developed show additional images of objects and people), as well as mental mediumship. He recorded his findings extensively for posterity.

Edgar Cayce - Cayce lived in the USA from 1877 to his passing in 1945. He developed an ability to enter a trance state during which Edgar gave detailed medical advice and information on a wide range of philosophical subjects. From 1923 he had a secretary who recorded the information given in the trance state. There are some 300 books on the work of Edgar Cayce who, it should be noted, was not a well-educated man. The information given is preserved by The Association for Research and Enlightenment in the USA, with groups in over 35 countries. The information he gave clearly came from a higher source.

The Bangs Sisters - Elizabeth "Lizzie" E Bangs was born in 1860 and her younger sister Mary "May" Snow Bangs in 1864, in Chicago (USA). They worked as mediums from a young age, encouraged by their mother who had mediumistic abilities. The sisters would sit side by side with a blank sheet of board supported on an easel between them. Without the sisters touching the board, Spirit Energies were able to produce high quality portraits and scenes, originally in about three hours but over the years this was achieved in twenty minutes. These large, high quality art works would have taken a professional artist at least 30 hours to complete. The colours were not from any identified man-made painting materials but were said to be like the colour dyes found on butterfly wings. There are many examples of these pictures on the World Wide Web and various collections. They also had the ability with Spirit to allow a person to write a question on paper that was then sealed in an envelope, with a pot of ink to one side. Spirit Energies were able to write and answer on the said paper. When the envelope was opened the answers were there and the ink was dry (there being no need for blotting paper for drying wet ink or avoiding possible ink blobs). The Bangs sisters stopped their communication work in the 1920s but left a massive archive of work that can be viewed today. It is interesting to speculate what the media would make of these art works in today's environment.

The Scole Experiment – In 1993, a group of four psychic researchers and healers embarked on a five year series of experiments in a séance room located in the small town of Scole in Norfolk (UK). There were many paranormal happenings in this circle, such as automatic writing, spirit photography using unopened film rather than a camera and materialisations. The experiments were held under strict scientific protocols and published in the book *'The Scole*

Experiment' - by Grant and Jane Solomon. The evidence favoured that the happenings were in co-ordination with intelligent forces, whether originating from the human psyche or from discarnate sources. However, being a scientific experiment the conclusion is in the proof recorded.

What's happening today? – There are mediums working in the public arena (platform and stage) bringing evidential proof of 'life after life'. There are many small groups of like-minded souls sitting in Home Circles, year in year out, receiving wonderful evidential communication from the Spirit Realms, together with spiritual philosophy through trance. Every week in Great Britain and other countries throughout the world, such as the United States of America, Canada, Spain, South Africa, Australia and New Zealand, there are Spiritualist churches holding services which include some form of communication from the Spirit World. Some of the spiritually-aware mediums are 'household' names and others are only known locally, but each and every one of them sincerely works with spirit to bring joy and comfort however it is needed.

Historical Documentation & Artefacts

There are a number of well-respected and professionally managed collections of historical documents and artefacts with known providence held by various organisations. The following are but a few of the main collections:

The Society for Psychical Research, the first learned society of its kind, was founded in London in 1882 for the purpose of investigating "that large body of debatable phenomena designated by such terms as mesmeric, psychical and spiritualistic and to do so in the same spirit of exact and unimpassioned enquiry" which has enabled science to solve so many problems. They have a library at their London Headquarters and a larger collection at the University of Cambridge (UK) of information relating to recorded spirit interaction with the Physical World.

The Spiritualists' National Union has a collection of documents and artefacts housed in a museum at their Arthur Findlay College, Stansted Hall, Essex. This is opened by arrangement and on special occasions.

The Spiritualists' Lyceum Union has a historical collection located on the top floor of Darlington Spiritualist Church, County Durham, Northern England (UK). This collection can be viewed by prior arrangement and covers the history of the Lyceum Movement as well as phenomena and Spiritualism experienced over the years.

Camp Chesterfield – Indiana Association of Spiritualist, located in Chesterfield, Indiana (USA), houses the Hett Art Gallery and Museum. This collection includes 25 Bangs Sisters spirit paintings, other spirit paintings by Professor Louis Carracciolo and Francis McVey. Among other items of interest are artefacts associated with the Fox Sisters.

Lily Dale Inc. is located in Lily Dale in the State of New York (USA) and is a Summer Camp for spiritually minded people. It has a museum located on the site housing an extensive collection of Spiritualist information, photographs and artefacts including items relating to the Bangs Sisters and the Fox Sisters.

There are various collections and special items of interest relating to spiritual phenomena in various Spiritualist churches around the world, including original Bangs Sisters spirit paintings in Portsmouth Temple, Southsea, Hampshire (UK). The Golden Spiritualist Church, San Francisco (USA) has a number of spirit paintings on display. These include two by the Bangs Sisters, around twenty four works undertaken by their founder Reverent Florence Becker (a well-respected physical and mental medium (1892-1970) and one attributed to the Davenport Brothers. The Davenports were American stage magicians who, evidently, according to reports at the time, had the ability to communicate with Spirit. Ira Erastus Davenport (1839-1911) and his brother William Henry (1841-1877) travelled the world with their presentations, including Great Britain and Europe.

There are, of course, a number of exhibitions/art galleries/tourist attractions of a dubious nature relating to the paranormal, ghost apparitions and 'things that go bump in the night'. The 'acid test' is whether this information has any providence or is just a figment of the imagination of the designers of these features. Unfortunately, there are too many people who will be taken in by what is often pure fiction and with little truth or background understanding.

The Development of Mediumship

The ability to communicate with the Spirit Dimension was probably an ability handed down from one practitioner to a suitable member of the clan as "The Medicine Man", "The Witch Doctor", "Holy Man/Woman" to name but a few of the titles given to those who presumed to have communicant abilities. In some recorded cases of people finding they had abilities, there was no 'sitting in development circles'. It just happened. Perhaps they were very sensitive people and just natural mediums. There is no suggestion that in times past these sensitives related their abilities to any religious dogma. However, different religions have a historical basis on received communication from the Spirit Realms and the particular interpretation to suit the environment, education and acceptance of followers.

It is correct to state that all religion is man-made and the concepts change over the years. Questions often asked relate to what is true religion and whether there is religion in the Afterlife. Every religion on this Earth has the understanding that there is a Higher Energy, that there is the ability of every human soul to progress with some perception of a Spirit World. Spiritualism provides an avenue of proof that there is life after life rather than a belief based on writings of philosophers and theologians and cultural inheritance. We are told by Spirit Teachers that those who pass with a particular religious conviction, or are agnostic, have the opportunity to review their understanding and over phases of learning, accept that every culture in the Physical World has a right to their particular opinions. It is evident that the spirit communicators who come to talk to us through trance mediums may well retain their Earthly persona, i.e. Monks, Sisters of Mercy, Oriental Mandarins, Native American Indians, Ministers and that they will use their Earthly experiences to explain their message.

What is Proof of Survival? Is the communication evidence Beyond Reasonable Doubt? Is the message conveyed from Spirit and not from the psychic sensitivity of the *medium*? Consider firstly what comes from Spirit as pure communication and what relates to psychic sensitivity. The word 'psychic' is often confused as it is a generic term for all types of communication that cannot be readily explained. Trained mediums expand their sensitivity and can become more aware of vibrations from people, buildings and objects. This can also apply to persons who have not trained as mediums. If you visit a dedicated holy shrine, a beautiful and peaceful church, or perhaps attend a concert, you come away from that experience with a special feeling - you could call it 'a feel good factor'. On the other hand, if you had to visit a prison or perhaps a place where a tragedy had happened you naturally feel despair. The same psychic feelings happen when you meet and talk to people. Do they resonate with you? Do you feel good in their presence, or is it the opposite? It is often quoted that when a medium starts to give a reading to a sitter the initial link with the sitter is on the psychic level and opens the door for a blending and the ability of Spirit to communicate easily through the medium.

What is anticipated as proof of survival provided by our spirit communicators? Names are always good proof, especially if the family name can also be given; relevant places, physical description of the loved ones, their work and interests and preferably the link between the sitter and communicator - be it family or a friend. Dates are good especially if provided with the actual anniversary. Can we expect spirit friends to remember these events accurately? Let us consider the special dates we can remember ourselves, such as birthdays and anniversaries, these being imprinted on the mind, can be recalled by the spirit energy. However, the writer has a problem with dates of passing; do we really think that when one passes the last act is to look at the calendar? Comments by spirit communicators on problems in the sitters' life and their frustrations together with health worries for themselves and others give a level of proof that the sitters' spirit helpers are aware of the problems and can offer some assistance, even if this just gives an understanding that they are not alone. It is often the smallest piece of obscure information that the medium is able to pass on that is the greatest proof of survival.

Proof of survival experienced by information given when a trance medium is communicating is often outstanding and gives an insight into the advanced knowledge gained by the spirit communicator. Physical communication can take many forms and prove the existence of another form of energy and this is explored later.

Mental Mediumship

This is where the medium or sensitive converts information within their brain vibrations generated by spirit communicators into pictures/objects, words, feelings, aromas, colours, physical movements and awareness of physical discomfort (suggesting the medical condition of the spirit entity at their passing). These vibrations can be received or interpreted as one or a mixture of the above-mentioned senses. The medium has the task of translating these effects into an evidential message that can be accepted by the sitter. It is always a matter of some debate as to the different ways Spirit makes itself known and the seeming limitations of the information given. It seems that when spirit energies connect with the physical energies they remember their last physical condition, which often is communicated as the way they passed and the medical condition/state of the physical body at the time. In general, spirit communicators give their forename when linking, rather than their full name. On occasions the family name is given but for some reason this is a rare occurrence. The interpretation of names that are not in the medium's normal vocabulary is attributed to the medium not recognising the vibration and perhaps they are reluctant to give a name that doesn't seem right to them.

Names of Guides and Mentors

Firstly, it is accepted that energies from the Spirit Realms we term 'Guides and Mentors' are very highly evolved souls with a great deal of knowing and experience. It is often questioned as to why so many people are given Native

American Indians, Sisters of Mercy, Nuns, Monks, Chinese Mandarins, etc. etc. A medium can describe an energy perceived with the following characteristics: Deeply religious; caring for others and putting them before themselves; not owning property; constant way of doing things; long flowing clothing; female. The probable interpretation is that the communicator, being from a religious order and making an association to the given information, then the name "Sister Constance" could be suggested. Once we have identified that spiritual vibration with a name, it can become the tag we use to identify the vibration. On the other hand, Spirit Communicators may give a name they wish to be known as (which may be that used in a previous incarnation). With trance communication, the spirit energy may well identify themselves and provide background information as to the physical life they experienced. This information can often be verified to an extent, especially where some research is needed and the information is outside the medium's knowledge.

Physical Mediumship

This is where the communication comes direct from Spirit, although there will normally be a medium who acts as the catalyst for the physical energy to merge with the spirit energy. This can cause a movement of objects, produce automatic writing, or construct a 'spirit' voice box within a trumpet (sometimes in a corner of a room) to allow direct voice to occur and also the manifestation of spirit forms. On occasions, physical communication takes place without a known medium being present – with the manifestation of objects, e.g. orbs, rappings, movement of objects and other apparitions - that cannot be explained other than by the closeness of Spirit wishing to make their presence known.

How is Mediumship Developed?

It would seem from the information available that physical communication generally preceded the advent of mental mediumship as we know it today. Nevertheless, there may well be evidence of mental mediumship that has been lost in the eons of time.

The development of mental mediumship by a medium relies on a number of factors, including how they are going to use the gift they aim to develop. Some mediums are termed 'Natural Mediums', meaning that they have from childhood an awareness of Spirit to some extent. These Natural Mediums often increase and hone these innate gifts of communication skills in a Development Circle under the guidance of a suitable teacher. It is said that everyone has a level of ability to link with Spirit and this communication can take many forms: Mental mediumship, physical mediumship, spiritual healing, inspirational speaking, psychic art, automatic writing, spiritual counselling and supporting others, to name but a few. When people decide that they would like to sit in a Development Circle they may have been told by friends, or perhaps mediums, that there is the potential to develop spiritual communication gifts in some form. On the other hand, the potential sitter for development of spiritual gifts may have an inner feeling that this is the right thing to do for their own spiritual progress and understanding, with the aspiration to help others.

Each Development Circle Leader will have their own particular system of teaching - which may or may not suit all potential mediums - and will be influenced by the leader's own Guides and Mentors. A Development Circle is a group of like-minded people who wish to develop some form of spiritual communication under the leadership of an experienced teacher. What type of spiritual communication will be developed seems to be outside the wishes of the student and in some way linked to the knowledge and experience of the potential medium's personal Guides and Mentors. There is no magic formula for the development of mediumship and some people sit for years without success. Development Circles normally include philosophy, to ensure a level of understanding appropriate for a knowledgeable medium. The Circle starts with an opening prayer, to invite Spirit to communicate at the highest possible level and to ask for protection from lower entities. Also within this prayer, each sitter makes a positive and personal affirmation that they will communicate with Spirit for their own 'Path of Discovery' and to bring help and proof of survival to those in need.

The students may initially be led through a guided meditation to attune with higher energies and where appropriate, the students may be encouraged later to go into their own form of meditation which may be accompanied by suitable music or natural sounds. Some Development Circles call this meditation 'Sitting in the Power' and this may last up to an hour, but the sitters need to be taught how to do this properly.

Another system which became popular in the 1960s from Oriental influences is the use of the chakras (discussed in detail later). The sitters are taught to enter a fully relaxed state by concentrating on various areas of their body, starting from the head, right down to the soles of their feet. Afterwards they link with 'Mother Earth', from where they bring up the (Earthly) energies through the feet and legs to open up the Root Chakra, then up again through the Root Chakra to open up the Spleen Chakra. Following this sequence, the opening up of the Solar Plexus, Heart, Throat, Third Eye and finally the Crown Chakra is achieved. This system seems to program the brain for the communication with higher energies. However, it is vital that the energies associated with the seven energy centres or chakras and the associated colours are understood - some teachers will use additional energy centres for enhanced attuning.

Following the meditation, the potential mediums will be encouraged to give off what they perceived. In many cases the leader will be able to tune in and help in understanding the communication. Some people develop basic communication abilities quickly whilst others must persevere with patience and trust in Spirit. At the end of the Development Circle it is vital that Spirit is thanked for their part in the session and that all the sitters close and ground themselves properly - initially under the guidance of the leader and eventually by themselves.

With **Physical Mediumship,** the development takes place in the séance room, which is preferably used only for spiritual work, being secure and safe. The room needs to be as soundproof as possible, must be fully blacked out and with a comfortable temperature. Ideally it shouldn't have a creaking floor or any high voltage cables below/above the room (the location should not be near a television/radio/ telephone mast as they give off an energy field). In addition, the seats should be comfortable, but not too comfortable.

Various devices can be present in the room to give the opportunity for Spirit to use these 'tools' to indicate their presence. These devices could include bells, sand trays, trumpets, tables, crayons/charcoal and paper, etc. A group of regular sitters will normally sit in a circle of chairs with the main medium sitting in the circle also. The main medium may sit in a cabinet that is just big enough for the medium to sit in. A cabinet is a square/round tent-like structure made from wood, card, plastic or cloth that is closed on three sides with a curtain at the front which may be opened during spirit communication. The purpose of the cabinet is to concentrate the energies around the main medium.

After the normal opening prayers and the request for spirit energies to communicate at the highest level possible, the process of building up the energies commences. In some Physical Circles a meditation is used, with everyone present devoting their energies towards the main medium. There may also be some singing of uplifting songs to raise the energies. Physical Circle groups may sit with patience for many months, even years, before any form of spirit communication on the physical level takes place. It may start with orbs being seen, taps and raps being heard and aromas being detected. Once these things start to happen the circle should acknowledge a presence and welcome further communication. The important aspect of all physical communication is that it must be intelligent communication from the spirit energies and not the manifestation of mortal energies (telekinesis). As the communication progresses, many things are possible and it can be a system of trial and error with the devices used. The main medium may be tethered to the chair by cable ties or similar. It is known for Spirit to remove the medium's jacket to prove that all matter is vibrations. At the end of the Physical Circle the group, especially the main medium, needs to relax over a 'cup of tea' and just take time to readjust to the normal environment and conditions.

The development of a physical medium seems to happen by experiment and gradual awareness, taking into consideration the following factors:

- Total trust in Spirit Communicators.
- Having a good understanding of spiritual matters.
- Physically fit (physical mediumship work can be exhausting).
- Wishing and desiring to undertake physical communication as the catalyst for the energies.
- Having a reason for facilitating physical communication for the benefit of others.
- Patience, as this type of mediumship takes time to develop and often follows the development of other forms of mediumship.

• All members of the circle are supportive, give their energies out to the medium and welcome the spirit communicators/operators.

What makes a good Platform Medium?

The skills needed for what people consider to be a good platform medium are very different to those for one-to-one readings. The platform medium, apart from developing the ability to communicate with Spirit in whatever genre, also needs these additional skills:

Charisma – Some people have a natural charisma, others work on this ability but it only comes across as true charisma if the sincerity is there. Many of the well-known mediums of the recent past and today have this wonderful gift that engages the audience within the first few moments of their talk or demonstration.

Presentation – First impressions are paramount; how mediums present themselves will set the scene. It's about the stature of the person, their entering the church or hall, walking with an upright gait, sitting upright, greeting with a 'happy face' rather than gloomy, thanking the chairperson for their invitation and the audience for attending.

Attire – Being dressed for the occasion (irrespective of how the congregation/audience dress) helps the mediums to gain respect and feel good in themselves.

Communication – The interaction between the medium and the audience is a skill that would be 'second nature' to a thespian. There are simple rules: Looking at the person being spoken to and if the comment could relate to the whole audience the speaker looks around the group. Before the medium starts to demonstrate they must always say that the communication is only possible with the co-operation of the communicators from the World of Spirit, or similar reference depending on the location and the anticipated understanding of the audience. In other words, the introduction will be different for a church congregation to a public demonstration in a theatre. The medium should always ask the audience to respond if they are chosen for a communication, with the sound of their voice and simple answers of "yes, I do not understand" or "I will have to ask others in the family" will suffice.

Vocabulary - The ability to have a good grasp of the language of the audience is paramount, but it is also important not to use technical terms or unusual words without taking the time to expand on the meaning. A golden rule for the medium is not to use words that they cannot pronounce, but this can be a problem when naming a place or a person - the answer is to say "it sounds like". The use of derogatory terms, slang or inappropriate language is unacceptable in a public demonstration. If the medium is aware that their communicator is using this sort of terminology then a simple statement, e.g. that the communicator had rather outspoken views or that their use of language was a bit ripe on occasions. Such a statement would get the point over without repeating the communication verbatim.

Engagement – The initial link with the recipient is vital to ensure that the person is not putting up a barrier, maybe due to shyness or stress. Much can be understood from the greeting words from the recipient, apart from making the link and ensuring that the medium has the right person for the message.

Preparation – Preparation for a demonstration takes a number of forms. Most mediums will prepare themselves mentally with a period of quiet mediation before the demonstration, to ask for clear, concise and relevant spirit communication. Excessive eating and drinking before a demonstration can make the medium feel uncomfortable - a demonstration could last a total of two hours without a break. Before an actor goes on stage, they will do some warm-up exercises with movement of the body and in particular, the facial muscles as these can help with the presentation.

Patience – There is a fine line to be followed. Some people have problems in remembering friends and relatives and others want more evidence before they will admit that they recognise the communicator. However, the medium needs to keep the communication flowing despite the delays incurred.

Understanding – A good medium will naturally, with the guidance of Spirit, be aware that there is a problem and be sympathetic, remembering always that it is a public arena and everyone is entitled to their privacy. In this instance the message may seem a little convoluted and only the receiver will fully understand.

Tactfulness - People often come to a demonstration in the hope that they will receive some proof of survival of a loved one, or to have some guidance of a major problem in their lives. The medium can only give what they are given from Spirit and may be aware that this can be affected by the person chosen for the reading putting up a barrier or only wishing to have a communication from certain spirit communicators.

Politeness – Rudeness from the platform when giving a demonstration is never acceptable, even if the recipient is being rude or derogatory to the medium. Some people think it's clever to act in this way but a good medium must work on a higher level and if necessary cut the link in the politest way possible, apologising for the link not being as strong as he/she would have preferred.

Limitations - It is generally inappropriate for a medium to give descriptions of Spirit Guides/Mentors in public demonstrations as this is not evidence of survival. Under no circumstances should a medium give any direct medical advice but can suggest spiritual healing and of course consulting a medical professional.

Special Cases - A medium normally gets an indication of where their link is in the room. If the right recipient is not identified it will become a process of elimination, where pieces of information may be understood by a number of people until there is only one person who can accept everything. If the chosen person is a child then the adult with them must be asked for permission before the reading commences. If the person has some form of disability then the medium will need to use suitable dialogue. The medium's spirit communicator appears to be more than aware of the particular condition and consequently the right help is given.

Sense of Fun – Spirit communication is linking with a joyous energy and the link should reflect this. The ability of the mediums to be lighthearted without being disrespectful (to the person receiving the message or the communicator) is a desirable skill. It's all about getting the balance right or having the 'happy medium'!

Finishing – To finish each message on a high vibration is very desirable; it can be a short résumé of the information given and whether the link gives love or respect to the person receiving the communication. At the end of the demonstration, the medium should always thank the chairperson or the organisers of the event for the privilege of having been able to work in their church. Also, to the audience or congregation, thanking them for their good vibrations and their assistance in helping the communication take place and hoping to see them again in the near future. In a public demonstration it is quite possible that there will be some people who need or desire further assurance and help. The medium could mention different organisations, such as Spiritualist Churches/Centres available to give support and advice.

What makes a good Private Sittings Medium?

A medium who undertakes private readings, or one-to-one readings, will hold the sittings in a secure and safe environment where both the medium and the sitter are happy with the location. It may be in a church or a home but the reading should take place where others cannot listen to the deliberations and at the same time eliminating any other external distractions. People who come to a medium for a private reading rightly expect the conversations to be totally confidential and the medium must make this clear before starting the reading. It is often the case that the person having a sitting has never had a reading before and they have a real need to obtain some form of reassurance from the spirit communicators working through the medium.

Mediums work in different ways and should explain to the sitter how they endeavour to proceed. Also and most importantly they should always state that all communication is an experiment and that anticipated results cannot be guaranteed, although the medium and his/her spirit communicators will do their best. Major advantages of one-to-one readings include having time to allow the sitter to respond, unlike the time pressure of a message being given in a public arena and others in the audience becoming bored. Another advantage is that the medium can be more open without concerns that the general public being made aware of confidential and private information. The requirements are the same as for a medium giving a public demonstration: There must not be 'fortune telling', proof of survival is incorporated in the reading and no medical or financial advice should be offered. Some mediums provide readings remotely, with the sitter providing some form of link. This could be a telephone conversation or a hand written note to the medium.

A good Private Reading Medium should have the following qualities:

Sincerity – To be able to ensure that the message being conveyed is truthful, using suitable intonation and volume of voice.

Confidentiality – It is most important that a high level of confidentiality is always maintained between the medium and sitter. If necessary, the sitter may need to be reminded that everything that was said was in confidence. If the sitter wishes to discuss the reading with others, that will be their privilege.

Empathy – It should not be confused with sympathy. A medium needs to give understanding of a condition and ensure that they do not become personally involved. By giving sympathy, there is a danger that the sensitive medium is affected by the conditions surrounding the sitter.

Support & Assurance – Although the medium will receive guidance on the message to be conveyed, he/she could offer verbal support and assurance whenever needed.

Advice – After the sitting is completed it may be appropriate to offer advice that may be of help. This may include the services taking place at the local spiritual organisation, spiritual magazines and newspapers, suitable books to read and others they can talk to for help. Again, this should remain in confidence.

Finding the right Medium!

Unfortunately, there are those unscrupulous people who offer so-called readings, energy clearance, fortune telling and predictions to the vulnerable, who may well be in desperate need of help - perhaps they have just lost a loved one who has passed to the Higher Life or had some sort of tragedy/mishap in their lives. These (unscrupulous) people are difficult to differentiate from genuine spiritual mediums that are

'Lightworkers' who only desire to help others in a loving manner. True, there are those genuine mediums who dedicate their lives to spiritual communication and make this work a commercial activity, charging a fee for their time spent communicating.

So how can a true and sincere medium be found who is in no way a charlatan? The following are good indicators:

Recommendation from appropriate sources such as Spiritualist churches/centres and knowledgeable friends/ associates.

Reputation of the medium is something that is only built upon success and satisfaction of sitters.

Qualifications given by various spiritual organisations that have trained, tested and approved the medium going onto their register.

Paraphernalia around the medium should be treated with caution - is it to enhance the communication, or provide mystic and paranormal illusions?

Payments charged should be reasonable and relate to the expenses incurred. (The fee may well be going to a charity or the local church).

Location of the place where the reading is going to take place should be clear and acceptable to the sitter.

Telephone Readings (known as Remote Readings) should be considered with caution. They need to be investigated as to what is being offered, by whom and at what cost. It is not suggested that everyone offering readings in this way are not doing it for the highest spiritual reasons. They provide a service that is easily accessible when meeting a medium face to face is a problem for one reason or another.

Taking the simple precautions suggested will ensure the medium is right for the potential sitter, remembering always that Spirit Communication is not a science but an experiment where the outcome cannot be predicted.

Addresses within Spiritual Services

The quality of addresses given within Divine Services is paramount to the total experience of meeting together to link with higher energies. One of the problems with Spiritualist services is that, in most cases, the Speaker/Medium is different for each service. Therefore, there is no continuity of philosophy given and possibly the same issues discussed, with just a change in explanation. The address may link with the reading chosen, or the hymns sung, but it is often the speaker's prepared words. What makes a good speaker is a combination of the trouble taken to research the subject, together with background knowledge and the ability to deliver. The general premise for a good talk is to start by telling the audience what they are going to hear about, telling the story and then reminding the audience of what the message was.

The tricks of keeping the audience attention include looking at different members of the audience, varying the tone of the voice and emphasising the important words in the spoken sentence. This can be achieved by altering the tone of the voice and using pauses in the delivery. The use of 'bullet points' or 'clue cards' as a list of the headings to be covered with perhaps important dates/names/numbers will assist the speaker. The inclusion of a related poem or particular words from a published document, if relevant, will help to get the message over. A speaker who keeps their eyes closed during an address will not engage with the audience, unless it's a trance address and the audience are told in advance what to expect. The use of jokes and funny stories is dangerous, unless the audience is well known to the speaker and will be in accord with them, otherwise offence can be caused. Using made-up stories to emphasise or explain a point is not a bad thing as long as it's not presented as factual information.

Additional thoughts on Physical Mediumship

Public demonstrations of physical communication from Spirit are very rare events. This type of spirit communication normally takes place in Home Circles and during courses or workshops, relating to physical activity. The term 'Spirit Operator' is often used in place of 'Spirit Communicator' as the spirit energy utilises physical (Earthly) energies to manifest various indications of the presence of spirit energies.

There are some people who will advocate that certain, if not all, phenomena witnessed is an illusion or conjuring trick. In the past, with mirrors and screens and today, with modern electronic devices, illusions for stage performances mimicking spirit communication can be very believable. To ensure that there is no suggestion of impropriety when physical communication is undertaken, certain precautions are appropriate. The sitters may be asked to leave mobile phones outside of the séance room, together with cameras, tape (or similar) recorders, torches, watches with luminous dials, cigarette lighters/matches and possibly shoes/jewellery that could make a sound and may be interpreted incorrectly as spirit activity. The medium may desire that he/she is searched for any possible devices that could be used to suggest the presence of spirit energies or physical activities by illusion.

The majority of the phenomena described below will take place in a séance room, in complete darkness. However, not every group will experience all the different modes of spirit communications, but just one or two types of phenomena:

Apport – It is an item of physical matter that spirit energies have moved from one place into another, i.e. the séance room. The theory is that every matter in the physical world (including the human body) is a mass of millions of atoms held together by a vibration. Spirit is able to alter, temporally, this vibration, controlling and moving the physical mass to another place, through solid objects at incredible speed, returning the mass to its original form. Apports are normally items of little financial value and typically semi-precious stones, flowers or trinkets, all of which will have some meaning to the recipients.

Automatic Writing – Paper and writing implements are placed in the séance room and Spirit is invited to write words or symbols on the paper. In times past, slates were commonly used for this purpose because they were widely available. There are many examples of this phenomena occurring with words often written in other languages, signs or hieroglyphics. **Sand Boxes** can also be used for automatic writing. They are small wooden trays filled with soft sand that is flattened out. Trays can be placed in a stack and one of the advantages is that any messages, or hand prints displayed on the sand by Spirit can be cast in plaster for posterity.

Direct Voice – Direct voice of the spirit energy is produced by two methods. Firstly, a trumpet device made as a simple cone constructed in card, aluminium or plastic with luminous spots on the top and bottom outer edges. (The luminous spots enable the sitters to see the location of the trumpet and its movement). Spirit energies construct a 'voice box' in the small end of the trumpet which they use to communicate. The second method is when Spirit construct the 'voice box' in an upper corner of the séance room.

Energy Lights or Orbs – They are like moving stars floating around the séance room and seen by all, indicating the presence of a spirit energy. It is known for one of these energy depictions to be seen to enter the medium's crown before spirit communication commences.

Hand Casts – This type of communication involves the spirit energy materialising a hand, or foot, in the séance room to such an extent that it is a solid form in every detail. Hot wax is then applied to the manifested form and allowed to set. The wax mould is used to produce a plaster cast, showing every detail, including the fingerprints.

Levitation – This term refers to the ability of Spirit to use physical energies to lift objects or people as a demonstration of spirit control over physical matter. One example of levitation phenomena is in table tilting, especially in the séance room where no one is physically touching the table when it moves. An exponent of this form of mediumship was Daniel Dunglas Home (1833 – 1886). He was born in Scotland and later brought up in the USA. He travelled extensively in Europe, demonstrating his gifts as a physical and mental medium. Home demonstrated the levitation of his own body and items such as a grand piano in public demonstrations, often in bright gas light. There are suggestions that this so-called levitation phenomenon was a trick, using a photographic camera activated by a thin cord when he jumped into the air giving the impression that he was levitating as the flash went off. However, there are many other accounts testifying to the levitation happening and the quality of his mediumship.

Can we speculate as to what is happening with levitation? We know what happens in space travel when there is no gravitational pull and astronauts can float around their space capsule. So can spirit energies alter gravitational pull by creating an opposing energy, just as two like poles of (same polarity) magnets reacting against each other? The movement of objects, including the ringing of physical bells/gongs in the séance room is not uncommon. The important thing is to establish eventually that there is some form of intelligent communication. The danger is that movement of objects can be instigated by the power of thought (termed **Psychokinesis – the movement of physical objects remotely**) which can be heightened unwittingly in the séance environment.

Materialisation – The showing of a spirit form, or facsimile, is brought about by Spirit using a substance called ectoplasm. This is exuded from the medium to build up an image for all to see. This type of phenomena requires an exceptionally gifted medium, supported by the energies of a dedicated group of sitters. The proof of survival is of the highest level, especially when the energy projected on the ectoplasmic screen is recognised and may be in certain circumstances photographed with infra-red cameras and identified against a pre-existing photograph.

Physical Noises – These are often footsteps, raps or taps. It is important to establish some form of code that indicates intelligent communication. The circle members need to convince themselves that raps and taps are not due to air in water pipes or heating devices switching on and off, or other external interference.

Temperature – In a séance a lowering of the temperature or cool breezes can sometimes be experienced, indicating the presence of spirit energies.

Transfiguration – This is the ability of Spirit to show a facsimile of a spirit communicator over the medium's face. It can be classed as mental mediumship, physical mediumship or a mix of the two. Mediums sit in semi-darkness but with a low luminescent dark red/ ruby light projected onto their face. The mediums place themselves in a light trance state and invite Spirit to make themselves known. Transfiguration may be accompanied by trance communication. Spirit may contort the medium's facial muscles, build-up an ectoplasm mask over their face to display the image, or it may be a combination of the two.

Some other forms of Communication

Auragraphs – These are similar to spirit artwork and depict information received by the medium. They are often drawn in a round shape with different sections which reflect the person's life, conditions and spirit links, as well as spiritual awareness. An auragraph is often produced by a medium as a precurser for a spiritual reading and can refer either to spirit or physical energies.

Cards as Aids to Spirit Communication - Angel Cards are normally printed on one side with a few words of spiritual guidance or a particular reference to a condition. After opening up to Spirit, the request is made that suitable cards will be chosen for the benefit of one of the group sitting for communication. The cards are shuffled and spread face down on a suitable table. The medium/sensitive giving the reading takes one or more cards for the person who is going to receive the message. The reader looks at one card at a time, reads the words and aims to expand on the message contained in the text. It is often the experience that the words are very relevant. The understanding is that the spirit operator has chosen the most appropriate card/s to assist the communication. Angel Cards are often used as a tool to develop mental mediumship and apart from the actual message, they give confidence to the fledgling medium.

Tarot Cards (also ordinary playing cards) can be used by individuals who have learnt the various displays or spreads and the significance of the pictures, with both sets of cards, the value of each, its suit and position in a spread having relevant meaning. The cards are normally dealt out by the reader in a particular sequence and their meaning is conveyed to the sitter as a reading. Some mediums use these cards as an initial link with the energy of the sitter before giving information provided by their Spirit Communicators.

Electronic Voice Phenomena (EVP) – This type of phenomena is achieved by spirit energies producing vibrations that are recorded onto an audio tape. The communication received may only be one or two words and the speed of the delivery may be very fast, so the recording has to be listened to a number of times to allow the human brain to comprehend what is being said. To produce this type of phenomena a battery operated tape recorder with a new tape (and the recording head cleaned) is used in a suitable location that is reasonably quiet. In addition, the experiment should not take place in close proximity to high voltage cables and radio/microwave transmitters as this could cause false recordings. As with all spirit interaction, the person or group must open in prayer, asking Spirit to communicate through the tape recorder. The recorder will be turned on for a short time and then played back to see if there is any noise on the tape. Remember that the Spirit Communicators may need to experiment to achieve results and it may take a number of sessions before they become apparent. It is not known if this means of communication is possible with the latest recording technology.

Flower Readings – In a way this is similar to Ribbon Reading (described later) and is normally termed '**Flower Clairsentience'**, meaning the ability of a medium to pick up the energies associated with a chosen flower. The person who is to receive the reading is asked to choose a flower, fern or greenery from the selection appealing to them.

The medium then takes the flower from the table and picks up the links with the sitter from the energy of the flower.

Orbs – An orb is a description of a ball of white light that is seen in normal light and is often captured on photographs. The lights are considered to be spirit energies.

Palmistry - The lines on the palms of the hands, the feet and fingerprints are unique to each person. There is an understanding that these lines, as well as the lines on the retina of the eye, are the vibration of the spiritual soul within the human body. From ancient times the lines of the palm have been studied and various indications relating to the shape, length and location of the lines suggest much about the person's persona.

Pendulums for Spiritual Communication – Pendulums can be utilised for the amplification of spirit communication which some developing mediums find an aid to their development. When used for spirit communication the pendulum will not identify an energy field but transmit spirit energies that enter the sensitive's crown chakra area and pass through the brain down the arm and hand to the pendulum being suspended. In the right circumstances, this will indicate Spirit is ready to communicate.

The pendulum is made from hard wood, plastic, glass, crystal/gem stone and should be personal to the user. If it's not new or the background to ownership or manufacture is unknown, it should be cleansed by placing it in the sunlight or other cleansing methods. After asking for protection and Spirit to communicate through the pendulum, the sensitive needs to handle the pendulum and to be aware of its shape, weight and also feel its energy. This makes the link with the sensitive's energy. It is then hung a the thread from the fingers to a length of about 25cm (10 inches) and by 'experiment' works well. The arm must be tucked tightly into the body to ensure the movement is not affected by 'Body Shakes'. It doesn't matter which hand is used, whichever is more comfortable (healers may prefer to use their giving hand). Spirit is then requested to indicate the movement of the pendulum for a **Yes** and then for a **No**.

The velocity of the movement will indicate the strength of the reply being given, so a gentle movement indicates a soft answer, whereas a vibrant movement indicates a very positive Yes or No. Thereafter, words can be spelt out and a code of communication established. It is also possible to ask Spirit to indicate areas where healing energy should be concentrated. This can be done by pointing a finger of the hand not being used at different areas of the persons seeking healing and looking for the indication by the pendulum movement. This system can also be used on maps to find information to explore crystal energy and their particular use - the opportunities are extensive.

Picture Concentration / Visualisation – A system used in the development of mediumship or spiritual awareness. The person who is going to receive a reading chooses a picture from a selection provided. The selection should include landscapes, seascapes, solar systems, photographs, still life, classical art, even abstract art, from which the potential medium can find inspiration. By concentrating on the chosen picture, the reader allows their intuition to come in and link with spiritual energies. This method can also utilise such items as small statutes, gemstones, crystal balls, marbles, craftwork or pottery as the object to concentrate upon. Care must be taken that the objects being used are not personal possessions otherwise this type of reading could be confused with psychometry.

Psychic Surgery – This is a form of Spiritual Healing, where the healer, under the influence of spirit energies, is able to enter the patient's body with their fingers and evidently remove diseased tissue. It is a rare form of healing that is practised by Spiritists in South America and The Philippines. Some reports suggest that the results and evidence could be questionable and therefore careful research should be implemented before seeking this form of healing.

Psychometry – It is considered that any solid object, such as jewellery, watches, combs etc. that are regularly worn by somebody, will absorb energies from the wearer. Psychometry, also called **Token Object Reading** or **Psychoscopy**, is the ability of a sensitive to read these energies. This process is often used in development classes to heighten the potential medium's intuition needed for spirit communication. In addition, some mediums use psychometry to attune with the sitter and work on the spiritual energies level. There are dangers that the object being read has energies attached from a previous user or even the place of manufacture. A similar system can be used for remote readings, where the sitter will provide a hand-written document for the medium to link with.

Rescue Work – In certain conditions, people, when passing to the Higher Life, find that they are at a lower level of the Spiritual Realms and desire to be helped to progress. Also, they may be interfering with others' progress by causing an attachment that is not desirable to ones in the Physical Life. One way these souls can be helped (those having difficulty in progressing, or are not aware that they have the opportunity to progress) is to communicate through a Rescue Circle.

Being involved with a Rescue Circle is not for the fainthearted and requires a highly developed medium or mediums working in the trance state with the full co-operation of Spirit Mentors who are trained in this type of work. The troubled soul is invited to communicate through a medium and one of the group (who is able to command a level of authority, e.g. experienced school teacher, magistrate or police officer) holds a conversation with the communicator. They will endeavour to understand what the problem is and suggest to the spirit ways of coming to terms with the difficulty, learning lessons and seeking progress of the spirit energy. The Rescue Circle, as a group, needs to support each other and ensure that they clear any negative energy before the circle closes.

Ribbon Readings – With this method of linking energies, the Medium will have a selection of various coloured ribbons, or it can be sample coloured cards, but they need to cover all the colours of a rainbow. The sitter is asked to pick three different colours that resonate with them. The medium then uses these colour selections to link with the sitter's energy and potentially link with spirit energy. The danger is that this can be purely the interpretation of the energy or vibration of the person and is, therefore, on the psychic level.

Spirit Artwork – There are a number of variations of this type of phenomena. The medium may be a trained or skilled artist who is able to draw an image of what they are seeing clairvoyantly and maybe give some verbal evidence at the same time. Artistic mediums often work with another medium, picking up on the same spirit link, to provide a drawing that complements the clairvoyance. In other cases the medium has very little artistic abilities, but under the influence of a spirit communicator is able to produce good quality pictures such as portraits, spiritual scenes, objects and other information that have some relevance to the person receiving the reading. In some cases the production of these images is very fast, faster than an artist would normally paint/draw, to produce the standard displayed. In other cases the image may be produced over a period of weeks, especially where the medium, under normal circumstances, is not artistic.

Spirit Photographs – Photographs showing so-called extras have been around since the invention of photographic processes in 1826 and do not seem to need the presence of a medium for this form of communication to take place. The photographic process has produced literally thousands of images of energy masses, objects and people that were not seen by the photographer at the time of the picture being taken. Some of these images of people have been attributed to departed souls and recognised as such. Great care has to be taken when discovering a photograph with extras as to the providence of the photograph. Was there any additional lighting or reflections that could have produced a mass of light? Were the photographs developed by professional technicians with clean chemicals? With digital cameras working through a computer, was there any usage of software to produce effects on the prints? When all the possibilities of something other than spirit energy being observed then the back of the photograph should be annotated for future reference. This annotation should also be used where there is some doubt of the authenticity of the so-called spirit extras. After all, the photograph could be discovered years later and misconstrued. It is common for white discs of energy, commonly called orbs, to be seen on photographs as extras. This is most evidential when the orbs are recorded on video devices and the energy masses are moving about.

In times past, it was common practice for people giving lectures on spirit communication to have photographs indicating spirit forms as teaching aids to help the understanding of clairvoyance. There have also been many attempts to produce photographs of 'spirit' extras in the past. The biggest con was probably when the writer and Spiritualist,

Sir Arthur Conan Doyle was taken in by the pictures of the Cottingley Fairies. They were just cardboard cut-outs of depictions of 'fairies', placed in the garden by two schoolgirls and photographed. Therefore, it is vital to ensure the best possible providence of any photograph with extras.

Spiritual Healing – This is a type of mental mediumship where the healer invites the spirit energies to instigate healing forces through the healer and allows those energies to pass through his/her hands to the recipient of the healing. Spiritual Healers should undertake formal training in learning the ability to link with Spirit, to understand the way the human body works (including animals where this type of healing is practised), the Code of Conduct as defined by the insurance companies (for their personal liability insurance) and their Healing Organisation. The training to become an Approved Healer requires not only the theoretical understanding but also the undertaking of healing practice under the supervision of an Approved/ Fully Qualified Healer.

Absent Healing is when healing thoughts are directed to a person in need by another (not necessarily an Approved Healer). There are various techniques for sending **Absent Healing,** which can be over any distance. To link with the person needing the healing the 'healer' may imagine a colour emanating from him or herself and another colour associated with the person in need. With the merging of these colours in the thought process of the 'healing prayer' energies can be sent. Another system to help concentrate the healing thoughts, especially where the person needing the healing is some distance away, is to imagine the journey and the location of the person. Where the person is not known personally, then the energies can be sent via the person who requested the healing for another. Some Healing Groups choose to concentrate their **Absent Healing** energies at a particular time of day so that the group energies combine for the greater good.

Table Tilting Phenomena/ Tipology - A number of people place themselves around a table, including the main medium. The sitters' hands are placed very lightly on the top of the table and spirits are invited to make themselves known. The communication received must be intelligent and this is achieved in various ways. The actual movement of the table indicating yes or no, together with the strength of the reply, also spelling out letters of a name or message. There is no standard way this type of communication works and it is for the circle medium to establish the code of communication of the table movements. The table can also be used to verify mental mediumship as well as having a conversation with the spirit communicator. Tables can be any size and it is not unknown for heavy ones to be moved at ease; there have been reports of a person sitting on the table when it moved – weight seems to be no obstacle. The use of a table is suggested but it could be any suitable object. *(We use a small bamboo table, which according to stories handed down to my mother came from the USA and was the first used for this type of phenomena).*

Unfortunately, in the past, especially in Victorian times when this type of phenomena was very popular, it was common for charlatans to move the table by mechanical means and to attempt to fool the vulnerable.

Tea Leaf Reading – Although this activity is not taken as pure spirit communication, some sensitives are able to provide an insight into the tea drinker's life. The tea is made with loose tea leaves and poured without a strainer. When the drink is completely finished, the cup is swirled around three times and any remaining tea carefully drained out.

The cup is then taken by the sensitive and the pattern of the leaves at the bottom of the cup is studied. The sensitive then relates what they perceive in the shapes and pattern of the leaves. (The pattern in the froth on the top of a cup of latté coffee can also be gazed at for spiritual inspiration).

Trance Communication – This normally happens when a medium allows spirit energies to speak through their voice box via spirit vibrations entering the mediums brain and becoming the spoken word. This is why trance communication is generally considered to be a form of mental mediumship. The level of trance can vary from very light, often referred to as overshadowing, to a deep trance when the medium will have very little awareness of the communication taking place. Even during deep trance, Spirit will never control 100% of the medium's brain.

The information given by the spirit control can vary from a chat about their present environment, to messages from loved ones, to deep and meaningful philosophy and in some cases the ability of the audience to ask questions of the spirit communicator. The best proof of communication from Spirit Realms is provided when the subject, or depth of knowledge transmitted, is normally outside the medium's experience. The spirit communicator will often use their own style of speaking, vocabulary and intonation of speech and gestures. It has been known for spirit energies to speak in other languages (see section on 'Universal Language' below) but this is a rare occasion.

One explanation for trance communication of philosophy is the ability of the brain to link with the medium's DNA profile and that of their ancestors and draw upon this knowledge. However, the level of the communication gives little credence to this theory.

Trance Healing – This is where the medium takes him/herself into a trance state and allows a spirit energy to undertake Spiritual Healing on a patient. However, the medium always remains responsible for the healing activity and this is one of the reasons that a trance healer should never be alone with the patient when the healing is taking place.

Communication by Vibrations – Universal Language

To try to understand how Spirit can communicate with other spirits and/or physical beings through a medium can be explained by a perceived universal language of vibrations rather than actual words. One suggestion is that the vibration for each word, in whatever language in the modern or ancient world, is a particular colour. (We know that there are countless colours in the spectrum which our eyes perceive, but there are other colours outside this spectrum). Examples are: A vibrant red for anger, a shade of pink for compassion, a vivid green for energy and a bright yellow for new ideas. So we have the basis for a universal method of communication with a certain colour for each segment of thought that could be locked away in our subconscious.

Meditation for Spiritual Awareness

Meditation is practised by many creeds, doctrines and religions with the purpose of achieving a state of spirituality or peace of mind. It can be used to programme the brain to become more aware, more vibrant and to be in control of the life-force. The general outcome of meditation is peace and tranquillity. This outcome enables spirit communication to take place effectively, especially in a learning group. Within a development circle, or workshop, a guided meditation is used to attune the members to a higher level where communication is more achievable. The person leading the meditation needs to speak in a soft tone but with a level of authority, directing the group in the desired path of contemplation. There are many written scripts for meditations that can be used and some people rely upon inspiration as they lead the group. Some groups also like to have a musical background/recording of the sound of sea waves, water rippling over stones in a river, etc. etc. to increase the peaceful conditions and to assist the reaching of the desired state of mind.

To take the group on a journey to link with Spirit, the 'Secret Garden' meditation is very effective. The group is taken on a journey from open fields through the woods, eventually finding a high stone wall that has a door in it. Each individual listening has their own private key to open it and enter. Once inside the secret garden, which is described with flora and fauna, the listener is directed to sit by the side of a clear lake. They are told to be aware of reflections in the clear water and to welcome the spirit energies that surround them. At this point the group is left in silence to endeavour to link with spirit energies. After a short time, the group are taken back, ensuring that they have locked the door to the Secret Garden, onto the open field. They are then instructed in firm intonation to bring themselves gradually back into the circle or meeting. One system is to count backwards from five with the instruction, at three, to become more aware; at one, to become fully aware, eyes open back into the circle. The group leader must ensure that everyone is fully back - some people may have gone very deep and need further words of encouragement to come out of the meditation while others may have just gone into a deep sleep. Only use words and never shake or touch the person who is reluctant to come out of the meditative state, as this may cause psychic shock of frighten them. People who suffer from epilepsy or have similar problems should not be encouraged to go into a meditation.

Another variation of guided meditation, but more advanced, is for the group to be taken on a journey to the Spirit Realms. The meditation starts with a description of gardens, woodland, seascapes or similar, where the group are guided on a walk, firstly being aware of the scenery and gradually less so, until it becomes just a haze. The group are then told that they are going to pass through a veil of pure light and on the other side, they will meet spirit energies. The group are then left in silence for a period of time to link with Spirit. After a while, the group is asked to thank their communicators and are slowly brought back to a full awareness by the reverse journey.

Associated Terms and Organisations with Links to Spiritualism

This section aims to give some information on terms used by people investigating the paranormal and groups of like-minded organisations:

Affirmation - A statement of intent that you repeat to yourself or in communication with Spirit by prayer

Akashic Records - Also known as the 'Universal Mind'.

Angel - A highly evolved spiritual entity.

Attunement *(coined word)* – Is the training of the brain to be receptive to energies generated from the Higher Realms. There are various ways of attuning the human brain to higher energies whilst developing mediumship in a circle or other event using a guided meditation, perhaps utilising the chakra energies or thought awareness techniques. During this training, it may be necessary to clear any negative energies/attitudes to assist the spiritual communication.

Astral Plane – It is considered to be the level of the Spirit Realms nearest to the Physical Plane of existence.

Astral Travelling / Astral Projection - The ability of the spiritual soul, the etheric body, to travel in the sleep state, to assist others or to learn some lesson for their personal benefit.

Aura - The energy field around the physical body indicating the state of the person. The term '**Auric Field**' is used to describe the perceived area of energy.

Australian Spiritualist Association - A Non-Profit, Religious and Charitable Organisation that aims to advance the Spiritualist and related Spiritual Movement and Philosophy, as a whole, in Australia. Their principles are the same as the Spiritualists' National Union.

Automatic Writing - The ability of a spirit operator to take over the writing ability of a medium to produce written works of spiritual guidance, philosophy and poetry. It is also known that music and lyrics have been produced in this manner. It could be said that Moses, being given the Ten Commandments, was the greatest recorded historical event of automatic writing, or in this case carving. References to a form of automatic writing to contact Spirit can be found in the records of the Song Dynasty in China *circa* 1100 CE (AD)

Cold Readings - A method of giving someone a message that they think is from Spirit when in fact it is a clever combination of the so-called medium making an assessment of the subject incorporating psychic reading of the energy field and conversation that gives clues to the conditions surrounding the sitter. By using this information and reading the body language and reactions a plausible reading is given.

Channelling – A term used for the energies/vibrations emanating from Spirit entities to influence a medium who is receiving information mainly as trance communication. This term is also applied to inspirational speaking, writing or artwork. A descriptive word that can relate to the channelling of spiritual healing energies from a higher source.

Clairalience *(coined word)* - The clear sensing aromas generated by spirit energies that can identify the communicator, such as the smell of a cigar, particular perfumes or not so nice smells.

Clairaudience – The ability of a medium to 'hear' a spirit voice, music or sound. The voice could be heard in one ear by Spirit manipulating the vibrations of the medium's inner ear – these vibrations are transmitted to the brain and understood as words. It is also possible that the medium may sense words in the same way as other forms of communication, i.e. by the spirit vibrations being transmitted directly into the brain.

Claircogonizance *(coined word)* – The 'knowing' that a medium has of/when spirit energy is making contact.

Clairgustance *(coined word)* – The ability of a medium to sense a taste that relates to the reading being given.

Clairsentience (coined word) – The clear feeling of spirit energies, that by training and experience, a medium can relate to and decipher. This is the sensation a medium has of feeling and touching that relates to the spirit communication being received.

Clairvoyance - The clear seeing of spirit snergies either through the mind's eye or by identifying energies by normal sight. It is the ability of a medium to see a spirit person, objects or symbols (generated by Spirit) and have some relevance to the sitter who can accept the given information. This word is also used as a general term for mental mediumship. (The term **Visualisation** is sometimes used in place of Claivoyance).

Chakras – Body - The seven energy centres, or Chakras, of the human body. Their generally perceived location and purpose are as follows:

1. **Root** is located at the point between the anus and the scrotum in the male - anus and vagina in the female. It is associated with the colour red and relates to basic raw energy but also keeps us rooted. The associated crystals are: Tiger's Eye, Smokey Quartz, Black Obsidian, Hematite and Black Tourmaline.
2. **Spleen** or **Sacral** is located approximately 15 cm (6 inches) below the navel. It is associated with the colour orange and relates to intuition and imagination energy. The associated crystals are: Carnelian, Red Jasper and Ruby.
3. **Solar Plexus** is located approximately 15 cm (6 inches) above the navel. It is associated with the colour yellow and relates to being the main centre for universal energy. The associated crystals are: Citrine, Black Tourmaline, Yellow Jasper and Sulphur.
4. **Heart** is located on the line of the heart but in the centre of the body. It is associated with the colour green and relates to pure love energy. The associated crystals are Aventurine, Kunzite, Peridot, Rose Quartz, Ruby and Watermelon Tourmaline. * (There is also an energy centre known as the '**Thymus**' between the Heart and Throat linking the two centres and regulating the energies. It is associated with the colour turquoise. This

energy centre is considered to be the pivotal centre between 'Mother Earth' and the sky/spiritual energies).
5 **Throat** is associated with the colour blue and is the energy for creativity, communication and the search for the truth. The associated crystals are: Aqua Aura, Aquamarine, Blue Lace Agate and Turquoise.
6 **Third Eye** (or *Brow*) is located in the centre of the forehead. It is associated with the colour deep blue or indigo and is the energy centre for clear seeing and perception. The associated crystals are: Kyanite, Lapis Lazuli, Sodalite, Sugilite and Amethyst.
7. **Crown** is located at the top of the scull between the two front lobes of the brain and the rear lobe. It is associated with the colour violet and is the energy centre for spiritual communication. It is the main chakra of the seven. The associated crystals are: Amethyst, Clear Quartz and Elestials, also Gold Topaz, Pink Topaz, Sapphire, Smoky Quartz and Tiger's Eye can be used.

Other schools of thought employ further chakras of the body and surrounding the physical body, also considered energy locations. They are generally classified in the following way, although the definitions vary:

1. Below the feet, linking to the physical Earth energy and balancing energies. It is associated with the colour silver.
2. Above the crown chakra and amplifying the power of self-intuitiveness. It is associated with the colour gold. The associated crystals are: Apophylite, Fluorite, Green Tourmaline, Herkimer Diamond and Rutilated Quartz.
3. In the palm of the dominant hand, offering a level of protection. It is associated with the colour white.
4. In the palm of the non-dominant hand, the essence

for this chakra is for truth and clarity. It is associated with the colour vibration termed 'clearn' (coined word) describing brightness, luminousness and the quality of being clear.

5. 15cm (6 inches) below the feet, this chakra is powerful for psychic surgery and embodies natural space. It links with 'Mother Earth' and is often described as the 'womb'. It is associated with the colour black.

Chakras – Earth – The seven centres of special spiritual energy are considered to be:

1. Mount Shasta - California, USA.
2. Lake Titicaca - South America.
3. Ulura Katatjuta, a huge rock - Australian desert.
4. Glastonbury – England.
5. Great Pyramid – Egypt.
6. Variable – changes with each age, currently Kuh-eMalek Siah – Iran.
7. Mount Kailas - Tibet.

Corinthian Church and Healing Association - This UK-based organisation incorporates: Meditation, mediumship, crystal healing, spiritual counselling, Reiki, colour healing, sound healing, card reading, church ministry and spiritual/absent healing.

Their principles are contained within the following:

We Believe: In God the Father and the Brotherhood of all life
We Teach: That we are responsible for our own actions in thought and deed and that only we can correct our wrongdoing.
We Affirm: The teaching and example of Jesus the Christ and endeavour to live by them.
We Know: That Spirit Teachers and Healers return to earth to help those in need.

Crystals – Crystals, or gemstones, have different properties depending on the way they were formed when the Earth was cooling down many millions of years ago. Crystals have natural energy fields and can also absorb energy vibrations. Some mediums and spiritual healers find that the presence of crystals (that have been cleansed), when they are undertaking spiritual work, can enhance the spiritual energy and communication with the Higher Realms. **Crystal Healing** uses various crystals particular to their known properties set out around the patient to enhance the healing energies of the healer.

Déjà Vu - The feeling that you have experienced something or a location before – often attributed to reincarnation in a previous existence.

Dousing - The use of devices such as 'V' shaped twigs or dousing rods to identify energies such as minerals and water below the ground level. Dousing rods can also be a matching pair of small, about 3mm (1/8 inch) diameter, metal rods in an 'L' shape with one leg longer than the other. The shorter leg is placed in a tube of a slightly larger diameter so that the rod can swing with ease. The tubes with the rods inside are held in the hands with the longer legs being horizontal. The longer legs of the rods will react and swing when a different energy field is detected. Dousing rods can also be used effectively to identify the strength and extent of the auric field emanating from a human body, or other form of life. The auric field will be limited or reduced when someone is giving off negative energies or putting a protection around themselves. A much larger auric field will be detected by the rods when positive energies are being generated.

Ectoplasm - A substance temporally exuded from a medium's internal physical body via an orifice, normally the mouth or nose. This substance is white and best described as a mist (which can have a rather nasty smell, said to resemble bad eggs). It allows Spirit to build up a face, figure, or object under séance conditions. The ectoplasm returns to the medium's body after the communication is completed.

Elementals – The term relates to the natural energies of Air, Water, Earth and Fire. Some spiritually-minded people will refer to these energies as being perceived as part and parcel of the whole of existence. The manifestation of these energies are described by some as the 'Fairy Kingdom', as 'Nature's Angels' and they are referred to by various names, including Fairies, Elves, Devas, Brownies, Leprechauns, Gnomes, Sprites, Pixies, as well as many others. These nature spirits are considered by believers as being governed by the Archangels.

The concept of Elementals is based on ancient teachings but there are many variations of understanding their spiritual interaction with our physical existence.

The term 'Elemental' is occasionally included in prayers when opening up to the higher energies and asking for blessings to include the natural world that may be on a parallel dimension to our own. It may be prudent to ask the question of a teacher/speaker using the reference to Elementals as to what their perception is of the meaning, as this term does not seem to have a standard definition.

Essenes - In Jewish tradition, the teaching sect called the Essenes, that flourished between 2nd Century BCE (BC) and 1st Century CE (AD), were noted for their abstinence and strictness of life. The mythology, recently confirmed in references found in the Dead Sea Scrolls, relates to the spiritual education of John the Baptist and Jesus Christ during the so-called 'Missing Years' before Jesus commenced his ministry. It is suggested that Jesus was a 'natural medium' and learnt to use these gifts with the Essenes to their greatest effectiveness. Dr Hugh Schonfield deciphered the Hebrew code of the 'Dead Sea Scrolls' as part of a team of scholars.

Etheric Body – The energy field around the human body (or other living creature) that mimics the physical body and extends beyond the actual body. Also termed the 'Aura' and as such is affected by the state of mind, physical condition and the positive/negative energies being generated by the physical being.

ESP – Extrasensory Perception relates to the heightening of the human inner senses, often relating to a person who has mediumistic abilities. ESP can also be detected in animals and birds in their reaction to particular conditions.

Greater World Christian Spiritualist Association – An organisation of Christian Spiritualist Churches and followers. Their beliefs are:

- *I believe in one God who is Love.*
- *I accept the Leadership of Jesus the Christ.*
- *I believe that God manifests through the illimitable power of Holy Spirit.*
- *I believe in the survival of the soul and its individuality after physical death.*
- *I believe in Communion with God, with His angelic ministers, and with souls functioning in conditions other than the earth life.*
- *I believe that all forms of life created by God inter mingle, are interdependent, and evolve until perfection is attained.*
- *I believe in the perfect justice of the Divine laws governing all life.*

- *I believe that sins committed can only be rectified by the sinner himself or herself, through the redemptive power of Jesus the Christ, by repentance and service to others.*

Their pledge is:

- *I will at all times endeavour to be guided in my thoughts, words and deeds by the teaching and example of Jesus the Christ.*

Their Headquarters are in London, with a number of owned and associated churches in the U.K.

Group Soul or Spirit Family – The perception that before coming to the Earthly Realms, we were an integral part of a Group Soul. Then on return to the Spirit Realms, the Spirit Energy returns to the Group Soul. The understanding is that the Group Soul, of which there are many, has a specific interest or role in the Spirit Realms.

The term **Soul Mates** refers to two or more physical beings that seem to have a special connection or relationship with each other that grows with time. It is sometimes considered that Soul Mates belong to the same Soul Group.

Higher Self - The spiritual soul or the spiritual part of the human body. The part of the physical body that is eternal.

Home Circles – As the term suggests, they are groups of like-minded people joining together for the purpose of linking with Spirit, with one or more mediums within the circle. The circle, or gathering, for spirit communication is held in a home environment, without necessarily being linked to any formal Spiritualist church or organisation. The type of communication experienced by these groups can be mental or physical mediumship, or a mixture of the two. The actual communication is often very evidential and can incorporate spiritual teachings from spirit mentors/guides.

(The) International Spiritualist Federation – This organisation, as the title suggests, has an international following that has an interest in Spiritualism in general. They hold twice-yearly events covering the development of various forms of mediumship and understanding of spiritual matters.

The Aim of the Federation is:

To reveal that Spiritual nature of Mankind which harmonises with Natural Law. (This forms the basis of Federation's Philosophy).

It's Objectives are:

To promote the advancement, by educational means, and the diffusion throughout the world, of a knowledge of the science and philosophy of Spiritualism/Spiritism. Such philosophy shall be considered as recognising the following Principles:

- *The existence of a creative life force*
- *The existence of a spiritual link between all forms of life*
- *Survival of physical death by the individual spirit Communication between individual human spirits and different levels of life*

Inspiration – The terms inspirational music, poetry, writing, speaking and artwork are often used when the author or artist feels that the basis for the work was beyond their normal abilities. The ideas may come in the sleep-state or in meditation - even that 'Eureka!' moment. Whether or not there was an influence from spirit energies being aware of the physical energies around or linking with the Universal Mind is of course a matter of conjecture.

Intuition - The instinct of taking the right action, or words to say - also referred to as the 'sixth sense'. With mediumship, it is the awareness of understanding and decoding a message, enabling a medium to give the correct information to the recipient of the spirit communication.

Karma – This word has its roots in Eastern ways of expressing Cause and Effect. Besides learning and experiencing, the latter implies atoning for our short-comings and not so good actions. It is reflected in various Spiritualist Principles of Understanding as personal responsibility, the need to come to terms with all actions - either in this existence or in the Spiritual Realms - and to learn from these experiences.

Kirlian Photographs – A photographic system discovered, by accident, in 1939 by Semyon Davidovich Karlin and his wife Valentina. It was achieved by the use of a photographic (metallic) plate connected to an electrical voltage. The resulting photograph of any living thing showed an energy field around the subject. This aura surrounding a human body or any other form of life can be read as to the conditions surrounding it.

Lightworker – A description of a person who aims and aspires to work with the highest possible spiritual energies as a medium or healer (in the broadest terms) for the benefit of others and their own spiritual progression.

Lyceum – The word 'Lyceum' derives from the Latin for 'School of Learning'. Originally this was the name given to the children's Sunday School associated with Spiritualist organisations. Their teachings were based on the visions of Andrew Jackson Davis and his description of the Halls of Learning in the Spirit Realms, especially for children who had passed at a young age. Nowadays, the Lyceum movement provides education and training in the principles of the religion and religious philosophy of Spiritualism and of good citizenship. It encompasses all age groups, from children to senior citizens, who desire to have an understanding of life's responsibilities and spiritual matters.

(The) Spiritualists' Lyceum Union (SLU) promotes the study and practice of Spiritualism as a Science, a Philosophy and a Religion, whose aims are to establish and encourage Lyceums throughout the United Kingdom for this purpose. It is associated with the Spiritualists' National Union. There are also Lyceums in the USA and other countries. The organisation of Lyceums in America dates back to 1860, with the growth of Lyceums in the UK in 1866. In 1890, the formation of the **British Spiritualists' Lyceum Union** took place - later to become the SLU, as an united group of Lyceums.

The word 'Lyceum' is also used as the name of a number of theatres and places of learning throughout the world.

Mesmerism - This is an early form of hypnosis developed by a German called Franz Anton Mesmer (1734 - 1815). Mesmerism was used for medical purposes as well as a method of inducing a trance state where in some circumstances spiritual communication happens.

Metaphysics / Metaphysical – The term 'Metaphysics' is on occasion linked to the title or the study of the understanding of both the physical and spiritual existence, attempting to give explanations. It is the study of natural sciences and the philosophy of being and knowing the theoretical principles forming the basis of any particular science – the philosophy of the mind. 'Metaphysical' relates to and deals with the understanding of what is considered abstruse and/or imaginary.

Materialisation - The vision of a spirit entity (or object) generally built up on ectoplasm in a séance.

National Association of Spiritualist Churches of New Zealand (NZA) - The Principles and their interpretation for the NZA are as follows:

1. The Universal Fatherhood of God
   A belief in the source of all things, whether that source is termed God, Unconditional Love, Divine Being, Loving Spirit, etc.
2. The Universal Brotherhood of Man
   That we all come from the same source and so are a part of each other.
3. The Communion of Spirits and the Ministry of Angels
   Our acceptance of the Healing energy that is brought through us from the spirit realms, to help all on the earth plane.
4. The Survival of Bodily Death
   The proof that our soul lives on after the death of our earthly body, through communication with loved ones who have passed over.
5. Personal Responsibility
   The acceptance that we are each personally responsible for everything that we do, say, speak or think.
6. Compensation and Retribution, here and hereafter, for all the good and evil deeds done on earth
   Our ability to experience the positive and negative aspects of life, in order to work towards a balance in all things.
7. Eternal Progress open to every soul
   The ability of the soul to continue to learn and grow, whether on the earth plane or in the spirit realms.

National Spiritualist Association of Churches (NSAC) - Based in the USA at Lily Dale.

The object of this Society is to effect a complete organisation of the Spiritualists of the United States of America into one general association, for the advancement of those purposes, undertakings and enterprises germane to the study of the phenomena, the promotion of the Science, and the promulgation of the Philosophy and Religion of Spiritualism.

Spiritualism is the Science, Philosophy, and Religion of continuous life, based upon the demonstrated fact of communication, by means of mediumship, with those who live in the Spirit World.

Spiritualism is founded upon a Declaration of Principles, nine in number, received from the Spirit World by means of mediumship. They provide a firm and tangible foundation on which to base the knowledge of Spiritualism.

NSAC's Nine Principles are:

1. *We believe in Infinite Intelligence.*
2. *We believe that the phenomena of Nature, both physical and spiritual, are the expression of Infinite Intelligence.*
3. *We affirm that a correct understanding of such expression and living in accordance therewith constitute true religion.*
4. *We affirm that the existence and personal identity of the individual continue after the change called death.*
5. *We affirm that communication with the so-called dead is a fact, scientifically proven by the phenomena of Spiritualism.*
6. *We believe that the highest morality is contained in the Golden Rule: "Do unto others as you would have them do unto you."*

7. *We affirm the moral responsibility of individuals, and that we make our own happiness or unhappiness as we obey or disobey Nature's physical and spiritual laws.*
8. *We affirm that the doorway to reformation is never closed against any soul here or hereafter.*
9. *We affirm that the precepts of Prophecy and Healing are Divine attributes proven through Mediumship.*

Ouija Board - A board with letters of the alphabet and yes/no areas printed on it. Used to communicate with spirit energies, using either a drinking glass or a disc with a hole in it (planchett), on which the sitters place their fingers. In the right circumstances, the disc or glass will move in unison to spell out a message perceived to be from Spirit. Generally its use is frowned upon as it can introduce spiritual energies from the Lower Realms that can cause distress. Often, users of the Ouija Board do not understand the necessity to open in prayer and ask for protection, together with closing down after using this device. The Ouija Board was invented in 1890 by the American lawyer and inventor Elijah Bond - it was also called Spirit/Free Board and Talking Board - as a harmless parlour game. The understanding that this is a method of spirit communication came later.

Out of Body Experience - Refer to **Astral Travelling / Astral Projection** above.

Paranormal – This is a generic term that was 'coined' in about 1920, to describe an event or experience that is outside the range of scientific understanding. This term is often used to explain perceived hauntings or phenomena, although these activities may, or may not be, attributed to the presence of spirit energies and could well be related to physical energies.

Planchett – A device for assisting with automatic writing and may either be used by one person or a group. A planchett is a heart-shaped flat piece of wood (or any non-metallic material). There are on the underside three small casters and on the top a clamp (or rubber grommet) to hold a pencil (crayon/pen/charcoal) in place. The medium places a hand lightly on the planchett and allows spirit energies to direct the movement of the device. The pencil marks found on the large sheet of paper placed below may represent words, pictures or symbols. With a group using a planchett, each person places one hand on top of each other's allowing the movement to take place, which will be in unison.

Poltergeist - A term used to describe an actual or perceived spirit energy, often associated with so-called negative/troublesome psychic activities.

Precognition – The ability to see into future events and situations (can also be termed '**Fortune Telling**'). The ability of spirit communicators to give information/advice on the future can be explained as the Spirit Community having links with our family and friends (also adversaries) and therefore have a more holistic understanding of our circumstances. An example could be that a lady who is pregnant at a very early stage and personally unaware of her condition (or has not confided with anyone at that stage). Spirit will be aware that a spirit energy has merged with the biological embryo and may convey this information.

Generally a medium under training is recommended not to give specific information on future happenings in order to avoid them to be construed as 'Fortune Telling' and not real proof of survival.

Psychic/Psyche – The word 'Psychic' relates to the personality of the soul/spirit/mind outside of the domain of understood physical laws and the laws of mental activity. When used as a description of mediumship, it can cause some confusion, as the word 'Psychic' has a slightly different meaning, i.e, a medium can also be a psychic, but a psychic does not have the connection or links with Spirit to convey a spiritual reading. Someone describing themselves as a 'Psychic Medium' may not be channelling information from the Spirit Realms but reading, amongst other things, the energy fields of people. In some ways the word 'Psychic' is better understood and accepted by the majority as a means of providing knowledgeable information about the physical existence, rather than communication from the Spiritual Realms.

A **Psychic or Mind Body & Spirit Fair** - An organised event aiming to showcase a wide range of mind, body and holistic activities, professing to offer beneficial outcomes. These exhibitors can include various forms of healing, aromatherapy, crystals, Oriental and Native American artefacts *(perceived to have a spiritual link)*, remedies, spiritual books, aura readings/photographs, handwriting analysts, psychic art, colour therapy, numerology, tarot card readings, psychic readings, spiritual readings, palmistry, demonstrations and talks on matters relating to mind, body and spirit. It is important that the stall holders/practitioners are fully conversant with the products/services being offered and the benefits suggested as well as any adverse effects, i.e. the healing code of conduct, which requires the healer to ensure that the client does not have any medical condition that may be affected by the healing energies.

Psychic Shock – In a trance, materialisation or physical session, if a medium is disturbed whilst under Spirit control, a psychic shock can occur. This includes the medium being touched - unless invited to do so by the Spirit control. Likewise, if during a séance undertaken in the dark or subdued lighting, a light is turned on, the sudden change in conditions can cause the medium some degree of shock and discomfort which may need some considerable healing work.

Quantum Physics – This is the understanding of how matter and energy function in our universe at the molecular level and even smaller microscopic levels. In fact, in quantum mechanics we discover that the entire universe is actually a series of probabilities. The theories and the proven facts are a way that some people endeavour to understand in order to create a connection between our physical existence and the Spiritual Realms.

Regression - A system using hypnosis techniques to remember possible previous existences of the human soul. It should only be carried out by properly qualified practitioners who ensure that there is counselling available if distress is encountered by the subject being regressed.

Reincarnation - The belief that the human souls (and other creatures) have the ability to return to the Earthly Existence from Spiritual Realms. Incarnation means an existence at some time in history, or now. The acceptance, or not, that reincarnation is a fact of eternal life is probably the most contentious discussion between theologians and ordinary Spiritualists alike. Some world religions believe fervently in reincarnation.

Our spiritual mentors have been asked this question on many occasions and have consistently given the following answer: "Progress in the Spirit Realms is an opportunity every soul is entitled to and to achieve progress and greater knowledge they need to experience different things in accordance with their chosen path of discovery". There are three opportunities:

1. To merge with other spirit energies and learn from their knowledge.
2. For the spirit energy to become attached to a person in the physical life to experience and learn with them - this is one way that souls who have passed at a young age can experience childhood.
3. To reincarnate back into the Earthly Existence, to experience things that are not available in the Spiritual Realms, such as greed, physical pleasure, physical empathy, parenthood, etc., together with modern technology, science and medical understanding.

Retrocognition (or **Postcognition**) – The ability to describe in detail an event, or scene from mind pictures, which was not learned from others' stories, books, films, television or paintings. The word was coined by Fredrick William Henry Myres (1842-1901) who was a founder member of the Society for Psychical Research.

Rune Stones – A system of stones engraved or painted on one side with 24 different symbols. A system of prediction dating back to Palaeolithic (at least 2,000 years ago) times in Northern Europe. The stones are held in a container and cast onto a surface in an East/West co-ordinate towards the Sun. The stones, which fall with the symbol face up, are read in accordance with meanings devised from ancient times, alternatively, three stones are taken from the bag and interpreted. Some people consider that the way the stones fall is influenced by spirit energies to bring correct information for the person whom the stones are being thrown for.

Scrying – This is an ancient art of concentrating on an object with a shiny surface and in certain circumstances producing a form of clairvoyance. The word 'Scrying' comes from the English word 'Descry', meaning to make out faintly and discover. This system of communication with higher energies is recorded as that used by the seer and prophet Michel de Nostradamus (1503-1566). When a **Crystal Ball** or other crystal is used for gazing it is termed '**Crystallomacy**'.

Silver Chord - A term used for the energy linking the physical body to the spiritual existence. It is said that this is the channel of energy that links a mother and child until the child is about eight years old. This link is also maintained between the mother and a child who passes to the Spirit Realms.

(The) Society for Psychical Research (SPR) – This organisation welcomes members of the general public, as well as students and researchers of all disciplines who have an interest in psychic matters. Membership of the society does not imply acceptance of any particular opinion concerning the nature or reality of the phenomena examined and the Society as such holds no corporate views. It was established in 1882 and has its headquarters in Kensington, London, UK. Apart from the research opportunities available there are also training courses and regular lectures for members on all aspects of the paranormal.

Soul Groups or Spirit Families – These are thought to be a group of spirit energies that link together in the Spirit Realms with common interests and activities to help others, both in the physical and spiritual existences, to enhance further their knowledge and progression. The term '**Soul Mates**' is used when two or more humans feel a real resonance and special understanding between them, which may be associated with being part of the same Soul Group. It is understood that we all come from a Soul Group to the physical life and return to that Spirit Family when we leave this existence.

Spiritism - Spiritism is based on the five books written in the 19th century called the 'Spiritist Codification' by French educator Hypolite Léon Denizard Rivail who used the pseudonym Allan Kardec. He reported on séances in which he observed phenomena that he attributed to what he termed incorporeal intelligence (spirits). Spiritism should not be confused with Spiritualism and it is based on the following five chief points of their doctrine:

1. *There is a God, defined as "The Supreme Intelligence and Primary Cause of everything".*
2. *There are Spirits, all of whom are created simple and ignorant, but owning the power to perfect themselves gradually.*
3. *The natural method of this perfection process is reincarnation, through which the Spirit faces countless different situations, problems and obstacles, and needs to learn how to deal with them.*
4. *As part of Nature, Spirits can naturally communicate with living people, as well as interfere in their lives.*
5. *Many planets in the universe are inhabited.*

Although there are groups and associations that adhere to Spiritism in various countries, it is most popular in Brazil. It is not seen as a formal religion as such by most followers. It is, however, an understanding that incorporates philosophy, mediumship and healing. One exception is The National Spiritist Church of Alberta in Canada which is classified as a religious organisation.

(The) Spiritualist Association of Great Britain – The **SAGB**, as it is more commonly known, has its centre in the Victoria area of London where they hold lectures, mediumship demonstrations (public and private), Sunday services, healing and mediumship development courses. The association was first started in 1872 and known then as the Marylebone Spiritualist Association with a history of holding large demonstrations, even Spiritualist services at the Royal Albert Hall on the Sunday of Remembrance weekend for many years. It became the SAGB in 1955. It is an independent organisation and has the following Seven Principles:

1. *We believe in a Higher Intelligence Who governs all.*
2. *We believe that personal identity and all sentient forms of life survive physical death.*
3. *We believe that continuous existence and eternal progress occur for all in the Hereafter.*
4. *We believe in communication with the Spiritual Realms.*
5. *We believe that all humanity is spiritually linked.*
6. *We believe that in the Hereafter, all must account for their actions on earth and will judge themselves accordingly.*
7. *We believe that all are responsible for the way they conduct their earthly lives.*

(The) Spiritualists' National Union – The **SNU** is an organisation with some 400 member churches/organisations, together with individual members, worldwide, adhering to the Seven Principles given mainly by the Spirit World communicating through Emma Hardinge Britton in 1871. These are:

1. *The Fatherhood of God*
2. *The Brotherhood of Man*

3. The Communication of Spirits and the Ministry of Angels.

4. The Continuous Existence of the Human Soul.

5. Personal Responsibility

6. Compensation and Retribution Hereafter for all Good and Evil Deeds done on Earth.

7. Eternal Progress Open to every Human Soul.

Their Mission Statement is:

To Promote the Religious Philosophy of Spiritualism as based on the Seven Principles.

The SNU offices/headquarters are in the grounds of Stansted Hall, Essex, UK. Stansted Hall is the home of The Arthur Findlay College residential education facility. There is also The Arthur Findlay Centre (non-residential) in Stafford, Staffordshire. Both centres offer comprehensive programmes of spiritual understanding and training courses for all levels.

Symbols – Mediums sometimes get symbols that seem to be personal to them and form part of the reading. It can also be a colour indicating, for example, pink for a family link.

Telekinesis - The ability to move a physical object by the power of the thought. Not to be confused by spirit energies taking control of physical energies to move objects.

Trance - The condition by which a trained and suitable medium allows their brain to go into a semi-conscious state permitting spirit energies to talk through the medium's voice-box. The level of semi-consciousness can vary from a light trance, often referred to as '**Over Shadowing**', where the medium is aware of what is being said, to a deep trance state where the medium will have little or no memory of the words being spoken by spirit teachers/communicators.

Transfiguration - The ability of Spirit to build up a facsimile of the communicator's face by contortion of the medium's facial muscles and/or superimposing a mask of ectoplasm showing the new features on the medium's face. With a suitable ruby light projected upon the medium's face, the recognisable features can be seen by most of the sitters. This may also be accompanied by trance communication, but in some cases the medium will do transfiguration and trance (or mental mediumship) separately.

United Spiritualists - An organisation based in the UK dedicated to the unification of Spiritualism.
Their aims are:

- *Unification of all people having a spiritualist belief and furtherance of the spiritualist cause.*
- *The promotion of quality mediumship, philosophy and pastoral care through ministry.*
- *Opportunity for self-progression with high standards for personal behaviours and way of life.*
- *High standards of qualification for associates who can qualify for membership through mediumship or by broadly accepting our understanding. Our belief is not just a religion, it is a way of life.*
- *Ordination of ministers. (Clerical attire being optional).*

Their principles are:

- *Belief in the continuation of life after physical death and in communion with the spirits of the departed.*
- *Acceptance that individuals are personally responsible for their own actions and spiritual progression.*
- *Belief in and reverence for an Almighty Being regarded as creating or governing the universe.*
- *Pastoral care through ministry to match the individuals' needs even if this is not aligned with the ministers' views or opinions.*

• *Confidentiality of information between associates and their clients.*

Universal Mind - (*See also Akashic Records)* - The comprehension that all meaningful thoughts, actions, understanding, philosophy and the good and not so good actions - in fact every possible segment of knowledge - is held in an energy mass, as a gigantic encyclopaedia of information. This information data bank is there for the Spirit Realms and ourselves, to access for our eternal progress.

White Eagle Lodge – This is an international spiritual organisation that was founded in 1936 by the medium Grace Cooke. White Eagle, who presented himself as a Native American Indian, gave through Grace, under trance conditions, many talks on philosophy. The Mother Lodge is located in Liss, Hampshire, UK, with other lodges in Texas, USA and Queensland, Australia. It also has centres in the UK, Australia, Canada, New Zealand and South Africa. The work of the Lodge is varied and enables people to develop their awareness of the inner light and to use it in a number of ways. Their particular interests are: Healing, meditation, retreats, spiritual courses, astrology and the philosophy of spiritual living as given by White Eagle.

In Conclusion

As the investigator delves deep into the phenomena of communication with the spiritual existence (or however human beings understand life after life), it becomes clear that the more we learn, the more unanswered questions arise. The term 'Beyond Reasonable Doubt' is used throughout the civilised world in making sure that the most appropriate explanation is accepted, especially when considering all that facts we have at our disposal.

The range of ways that Spirit communicates and the perceived standard of the mediums' abilities cause much discussion. Firstly, the range of types of communication has changed over the years that we have reliable records for. There is an emphasis on forms of trance communication for the great philosophy writers and physical communication through what we may consider today as rather basic, e.g. raps and taps.

Today the main avenue of spirit communication is by mental mediumship with less physical communication. We have to accept that mental mediumship is a partnership between the medium and their spirit communicators. The type of mental mediumship that the medium develops seems to be the one desired by the spirit communicators, be it the ability to see, hear or sense their communication.

We need to consider what is happening with spirit communication. When the spirit energy links with the Physical World, the memory is triggered to recall the vibration of the discarded physical body at the time of passing. This is an explanation as to why so much clairvoyance seems to relate to the suffering, aches and pains at the time of transition. Names given invariably relate to the first name and rarely to the family name. If we accept that spirit energies are identified as a unique vibration, a name is perhaps unimportant to the message they want to convey. On rare occasions, the medium will be told of the name the spirit entity wishes to talk to. If, for example, a mother or father is making the link, then common sense suggests that they should be able to say who they want. There are many questions that the serious investigator finds inexplicable and we have to accept that some things are beyond our comprehension.

Philosophy given by various Spirit Teachers, now and in the past, may seem to contradict each other. One explanation is that the teaching was right and suitable for the time and the audience, whether presented in written word, public demonstration or trance communication. The way the teaching is given and the words used relate clearly to the requirements of the audience and their level of understanding, although the basic message should remain the same.

What are the futures of spiritual understanding and the provision of ways of accessing a spiritual path in the most complete way possible? The future of Spiritualist churches and organisations, as we know them today, relies on the quality of the product being offered and the ability to change with the times in a proactive way. The professional way the services are conducted is important. This should encompass a blend of knowledgeable people who have invested much time and energy on their own path of discovery and the desire to assist others in their spiritual understanding. The quality of mediumship must be developed and maintained to meet the aspirations of proof beyond reasonable doubt. The development of mediumship for spiritual awareness must go hand in hand with a clear and concise understanding of the philosophy of Spiritualism in whatever form it takes.

Those mediums who are skilled, confident and brave enough to demonstrate their mediumistic abilities (in churches, theatre shows and on television/radio recordings) must able to command respect and that they are linking with higher energies for the benefit of the audience. It is possible that some attendees will be ignorant or doubtful of the true mechanics of spirit communication and may well consider it an entertainment.

Spirit communication has been a part of the physical existence since the life-force on our Earth evolved. We have much evidence of spirit communication and even more written into ancient folklore and legends, some of which have an element of truth of the interest that Spirit has and always will have in the physical existence. There is no reason to suggest that this level of interest will not continue. As man becomes more aware of the spiritual element of the physical existence, whatever religion, creed or understanding they follow, Spirit will be there to support in the most appropriate way – this is evolution in its most holistic form!

The most important lesson, in my opinion, is to keep always an open mind on spiritual matters and spirit communication. Although there are so many different understandings throughout our physical existence, there is also an element of truth in each way of thinking. However, some teachings may have been lost from the original concept and beliefs. It is common knowledge that some truths have been manipulated for the benefit of the ruling bodies and controlling the masses by religious leaders, priests and theologians, clouding the true lessons and spiritual responsibilities.

I am genuinely amazed at what Spirit puts into my head when giving a reading. It's often the most obscure detail that is real proof for the sitter. Recently, I was aware of the sitters' father communicating, referring to his toes being misshapen – this was a family trait that had been passed down the generations. The lady then agreed that her toes and those of her daughter's had the same problem as her father's, confirming without doubt he was there for her. Clearly Spirit performs its miracles in a wonderful way!

Each and every one of us has different needs and inner desires for our spiritual well-being. The following factors could influence our path of understanding and way of thinking - they are given in no particular order as everyone's priorities will be different:

- **Family Upbringing** – Was the family/guardians loving, materialistic, religious, selfish, supportive of others, open in thought, closed ideas/ideals, generous etc.?

- **Peer Pressure** – Are you influenced by others around you, e.g. friends, work colleagues, managers, customers/clients?
- **Experiences** – Has there been a major event or a series of minor events that have changed your way of thinking?
- **Education** – Have your studies influenced the way you think? Are you analytical, or frustrated by lack of education?
- **Work Experiences/Skills** – Do the experiences of work affect your spirituality, either for the good or not so good?
- **Gender** - The male and female in general terms are fundamentally different in the way they offer comfort, support, parenthood, sympathy and love.
- **Race** – The ethnic background will have an effect, especially where there are inbred creeds and lifestyles.
- **Aspirations** – Each one of us has aspirations that may influence our path of discovery in this physical life. Do we really have clear goals and aspirations for our spiritual development?
- **Mediumistic Abilities** – The development of mediumship brings a clearer understanding and application of the abilities and limitations of spirit communication, which can change a medium's whole way of thinking.
- **Opportunities** – Do you take the opportunities that come your way? They may be there for your development.
- **Age** – There comes a time in everyone's physical life when thoughts become more concentrated on the purpose of life. It may happen in the formative years, or in later life. Some people may term this as 'Seeing the Light'.

- **Responsibilities** – The requirements of family life and career development may well overwhelm and leave little time for you to think outside the narrow constraints that are part of your current lifestyle.

These suggested ways of understanding our own needs may (by the very nature of the human being) vary from one person to another. In addition, other factors may influence, enhance or limit our spiritual path of understanding.

Every effort has been made in preparing this book to use the most common terms and straightforward explanations. Some of the words used are not in common English language and may have been *coined* when no other word was available. Therefore, such words are not in the full and complete *The Oxford English Dictionary*. Much deeper explanations can be found where the use of complex scientific explanations and theories are suggested and may well cause more confusion than enlightment.

Everyone has a different level of understanding and threshold of acceptance. The aim has been to keep the explanations simple and logical, allowing for further thought and investigation.

Seeking further explanations and knowledge needs to come from trusted and reliable sources. The majority of the spiritual organisations and many churches publish their own World Wide Web pages that reflect their particular understanding and doctrine and as such can be considered to be reliable. Most of these organisations have their own published books and leaflets. There are a number of spiritual/psychic newspapers and magazines around the world as commercial and semi-commercial publications. Some, however, can tend to sensationalise the paranormal and not really concentrate on spiritual knowledge and support. There is a vast library of books written in the past (some still currently available) on every conceivable variation of perceived spiritual knowledge/understanding. You only have to enter any bookshop to find a section on 'Mind/Body/Spirit' with some specialist etheric bookshops around the world and on the websites.

Try:

www.ghostcircle.com/ebooks (The Science of Physical Mediumship) & **www.survivalebooks.org** You can download free spiritual e-books, some no longer in print.

It is clear that the ways our spirit friends will communicate in the future is going to change as we become more spiritually and scientifically aware. Perhaps this will be to ensure that their evidential communication is 'Beyond Reasonable Doubt' and provide a greater level of understanding and acceptance of the truths.

So finally, we all have our own 'Path of Discovery', our own lessons to learn and to come to our own conclusions. I hope this book goes some way to providing a clearer understanding and perhaps enthuses the need to ask more questions ensuring, as always, the balance of proof is 'Beyond Reasonable Doubt'.

NOW IS YOUR CHANCE TO RUN YOUR OWN SPIRITUAL WORKSHOP

Facilitator's Notes

The aim of the Training Plan is to suggest a structured presentation entitled '**Beyond Reasonable Doubt**' that will be complemented by the book *Beyond Reasonable Doubt,* which will form part of the training. A personal copy can be presented to each student attending as an integral part of the learning experience. The actual presentation will largely depend on the knowledge of the presenter and the level of understanding of the group of trainees. This presentation material is not biased towards any particular Spiritualist of spiritual organisation but endeavours to give a wide spectrum of information.

The training time can vary from a two to four hour presentation and will depend on the number of exercises used. The training is split into 'themes' and could, therefore, be undertaken over a number of sessions as part of a Development Circle background training, which is vital for a prospective medium's understanding.

Charging for workshops, apart from covering the incurred costs, has the advantage of pre-sale of tickets and knowing the numbers attending. Paying a reasonable price for the workshop has certain advantages, including the heightened expectation of the students and in a way the desire for value for money and the time invested.

Linking the workshop with a buffet lunch or high tea can be advantageous. Also linking the workshop with a guest presenter to follow the workshop can create interest. Perhaps this could be a Psychic Artist, transfiguration demonstration, trance demonstration or well-respected Mental Medium. It could also be something completely different, such as a musical or poetry evening.

Training Plan

Theme A - Introduction

1. Introduction & welcome – Who you are and that you expect to get as much, if not more, by this training experience, as the group.
2. Housekeeping – Fire exits, toilets, programme, timing, refreshments and please turn off or mute mobile/cell 'phones!
3. Aim – To provide a wide spectrum of information on Spiritual matters – some participants may already be familiar with, whilst others may be less aware. Invite the group to add to your own experiences and knowledge for the benefit of the whole group.
4. Who are you? (the learners) – What is their background and what do they want and expect from the day? (This information could be written up on a flip chart or suspended sheet of paper and as the goals are covered - ticked off). At this stage it is worth saying that if something comes up where collectively the answer is not known, then you (the presenter) will aim to seek an answer and advise the group in due course.
5. Opening up – If you are going to undertake spiritual communication exercises, open up and seek protection, asking for the highest possible spiritual energies to work with the whole group.
6. What is evidence? – Ask your group to say what they consider to be the most effective and acceptable evidence of the communication from spirit to provide proof of survival. Depending on the group size you could ask for one or more examples. Look for the similarities and anything that has been missed.

7. What Spiritualist/spiritual organisation is the church/group affiliated to? What other groups are there worldwide and how do they differ?

Theme B - Mental Mediumship

1. What is a Psychic (as one who reads psychic energy)?
2. What is a Spiritual Medium (as one who is able to transmit information from spirit energy)?
3. What is mental mediumship?
4. How is spiritual mediumship developed? (Natural mediums, childhood communication with unseen friends and events that have triggered communication or desires to become a serving medium).
5. What makes a good platform medium? (Ask the group what they think).
6. What makes a good private – One to One – sitting medium?
7. How trance communication is achieved. What are the benefits and possible criticisms?
8. What is Cold Reading?

Theme C – Physical Mediumship

1. What is Physical Mediumship (compared to mental mediumship)?
2. What is a Physical Medium and how do they develop this particular ability?
3. Examples of past evidence (with providence) of physical communication (the World Wide Web has many pictures available).

Theme D – Historical Evidence of Spirit Communication

1. Biblical references in the New and Old Testaments.
2. References in other religions of spirit teachings that have influenced ways of thinking.
3. References with providence of spirit communication, either by physical activity or trance communication.

Theme E – What of the Future?

1. What do you want (the group) for a satisfying, progressive educational ability to communicate with ease with friends and family who have progressed to the life after life, companionship, refuge etc. etc?
2. How can the services be improved/modernised?
3. How can Spiritualism/spiritual understanding go forward?
4. What makes a good speaker and excellent address?
5. Close in prayer – especially if exercises are used.
6. Give out personal copies of *Beyond Reasonable Doubt.*

Possible Exercises - To incorporate within (all, some or others) the workshop. In all cases, make the statement that we are going to ask our **Spirit Friends** to work with us for the result we want to achieve (state what result you want). Remember, all communication is an experiment and some may work better than others – but have faith in Spirit!

Colours – Aiming to demonstrate that communication can be a colour vibration. Materials – sheets of coloured paper, at least six pairs of each colour and one blindfold. A person from the group is blindfolded and given one of the coloured sheets from the selection. All the colours are placed on a table, including the pair to the sheet being held by the reader. They are then asked to identify the same colour energy, sheet of paper, from the papers laid out.

Angel Cards – For spiritual readings. The pack of cards are laid on a table face down and mixed up. The group are split into pairs, one person being the reader and the other the accepter. The reader chooses up to three cards from the pack, spread out, then uses the words on the cards as the starter for giving a short reading by linking with Spirit.

Mystery Envelopes – A number of photographs or pictures are prepared before the event and placed into identical envelopes, the envelopes being marked with a simple A, B, C etc. The envelopes will be passed around the group and they will be asked to write down their impressions. Each envelope is opened separately and the group are asked what they wrote down – consider the similarities and how the impressions related to the subject matter of the photograph or picture.

Pendulums for Spiritual Communication – Each person needs to be supplied with a pendulum but this does not need to be an expensive hand-crafted object. You can use a large nut such as a chestnut or almond with a thread attached or perhaps a tumbled polished stone with a suitable 'finding' glued on to attach the thread.

Tea Leaf Reading – For a spiritual connection.

Visualisation – Provide a suitable painting (where you can look into the detail and use the imagination). Ask the group to look at the picture and take their minds on a journey of discovery. This can also be done with each person working on their own with a selection of pictures available - old calendar pictures are ideal. Each person picks a picture that appeals to them and senses what they pick up intuitively or by spirit communication.

Meditation – This needs to be a lead meditation with aims and objectives.

Energy Generator – Ask the group to sit in a comfortable position and relax. Ask them to place one palm of the hand face to face with the other and to move them slowly in a circular motion; after a short while the movement will become difficult and the palms will stick together. At this stage the palms are slowly placed on the brow and the energy, the healing energy, will be felt. Ask them to stroke the brow and appreciate the energy. Then tell the group to take their hands down and shake them to clear the energy. This is a quick fix for eye strain, headaches, or any other part of the body that needs a little TLC.

Presenters Hits

- Always prepare more material than you are going to need.
- Have your programme in front of you.
- Be prepared to add and modify the presentation, especially if you don't know your audience in advance.
- The use of flip charts can be enhanced by writing bold headings beforehand and putting notes in pencil for your benefit, especially relevant dates and unusual spelling.
- Prepare yourself before the presentation by relaxing and exercising the facial muscles, the arms and legs.
- Use hecklers or people who constantly interfere to your advantage.
- If you don't know the answer, offer to find out if possible. A great deal of information is contained within the book.
- Advise on books, magazines and other training available, to assist in each and everyone's Journey of Discovery
- Always thank your audience and enjoy the event.

BEYOND REASONABLE DOUBT

—

Corrections and Additional Information

Corrections

Page 7 Should be Brenda Harrington not Harrison

Page 55 Should be skull and not scull – relating to the crown chakra location

Additional Information

The Spiritualist Lyceum Union - museum incorporated into the Britten Museum at Arthur Findlay College - Stansted Hall.

The Unitarian Society for Psychical Studies is a special group interested in phenomena in their various forms of investigation into spirit activities. Its main objective is to encourage the study of physical phenomena in all aspects with a critical and open mind. The group has been in existence for the last 45 years and is linked to the General Assembly of Unitarians and Free Churches which have an ethos of open-mindedness and the personal development of everyone's spiritual understanding within a Christian envelope of awareness. This society publishes its journal twice a year, presents a lecture to their Annual General Assembly, and organises other events such as their Annual USPS Conference. (For further background look at www.unitariansocieties.org.uk and follow the links to Society for Psychical Studies; alternatively the Journal Editor is David Taylor can be contacted via e-mail editorusps@yahoo.co.uk

The Quaker Fellowship for After-Life Studies has a special interest in spirit communication within the ethos of the Quaker way of life and holds various events. Web page www.quakerfelowshipforafterlifestudies.co.uk for further information.

Scottish Society for Psychic Research is a registered educational charity dedicated to investigating the paranormal in Scotland in a scientific manner and hosting public lectures & responding to public requests to investigate paranormal phenomena. Web page www.sspr.co.uk for further information.

Woodlands Sanctuary Foundation based in Australia. Publishers of the on-line *Psypioneer* Journal and a vast accessible archive covering many aspects of spiritual knowledge, via search engine. Founded in 1995, the object of the Foundation is to be an educational organisation for the advancement and development of spiritual awareness. Web page www.woodlandway.org for all the information and access to the Journal and archives.

The Pioneer – Bi-monthly electronic publication by Paul J. Gaunt Editor of Pioneer & Curator of Britten Museum and Library @ Stansted Hall. Historical articles on history of Spiritualism available free of charge at pioneer@snu.org.uk

The American Society for Psychical Research is the oldest psychical research organization in the United States. For more than a century, it's mission has been to explore extraordinary, or as yet unexplained, phenomena that have been called psychic or paranormal, and their implications for our understanding of consciousness, the universe and the nature of existence. How is mind related to matter, energy, space and time? In what unexplained ways do we interconnect with the universe and each other? The ASPR addresses these profoundly important and far-reaching questions with scientific research and related educational activities including lectures, conferences and other information services. Web page www.aspr.com for further information.

Hafan Y Coed Psychic and Spiritual Development Centre located in South Wales offering courses and one- day workshops on trance mediumship, transfiguration, psychic development, mediumship, clairvoyance, meditation, psychometry, psychic art and spiritual art; one- day psychic development workshops and other forms of spiritual progress. Their aim is serving the spiritual world and helping others develop and grow spiritually. An independent organisation.
Web page www.hafanycoed.com for further information.

The College of Psychic Studies – based in London and founded in 1884, the College is a beacon of light and learning for those seeking to explore a consciousness beyond matter. Web page www.collegeofpsychicstudies.co.uk for further information.

Association for the Scientific Study of Anomalous Phenomena a U.K. based organisation investigating the paranormal and publishing their findings.
Web page www.assap.ac.uk for further information.

Psychic News archive from 1932 – libguides.lib.umanitoba.ca/psychicnews

There are many other groups around the world – some lasting a short time, others becoming established organisations. The amount of information gathered by these groups is immense and in most cases accessible as published papers and on the Internet. Although the organisations listed are the more well-known and in the English, there are others that publish in French, Spanish, Portuguese (Brazilian), Icelandic, Scandinavian languages.